How To l
By D

Fighter's Mindset

Alain Burrese

TGW BOOKS
Missoula, Montana

Also by Alain Burrese:

Books:

Lost Conscience: A Ben Baker Sniper Novel
Hard-Won Wisdom From The School Of Hard Knocks
Tough Guy Wisdom
Tough Guy Wisdom II: Return of the Tough Guy
Tough Guy Wisdom III: Revenge of the Tough Guy

DVDs:

Hapkido Hoshinsul
Streetfighting Essentials
Hapkido Cane
Lock On: Joint Locking Essentials vols. 1-5
Restraint, Control & Escort Techniques vols. 1 & 2

Print ISBN: 978-1-937872-09-0
eBook ISBN: 978-1-937872-08-3

Published by TGW Books, a division of
Burrese Enterprises, Inc.
Missoula, MT 59801, USA

Cover design by Alain Burrese & Bryan Whitney.

Contents

Develop A Fighter's Mindset

"If you are going to win any battle, you have to do one thing. You have to make the mind run the body. Never let the body tell the mind what to do…"

- General George S. Patton, Jr.

Martial art training, reality based self-defense training, and any other program of physical personal protection won't help you one bit if you don't have the proper mindset. Without developing the fighter's mindset, a person will fail to effectively use the training from such programs. And the person with the fighter's mindset will often prevail even if the person has had no other training. Going berserk on an attacker with everything you have can be just as effective, sometimes even more effective, than so called fighting systems. But you will only do this when you have the proper mindset.

"The Fundamental principle of surviving violence is mental. Not physical, not gadgetry, but mental preparation, mind-setting.

- Stanford Strong

It is for this reason that I believe that developing your mindset, a fighter's mindset, or a warrior's mindset, is the most important ingredient to protecting or defending yourself. If you develop the mindset that I set forth in this book, you will be able to protect yourself better than before. You will be able to defend yourself better. The principles of mindset that I share here will be the foundation of your self-defense training and protection strategies that keep you and your loved ones safe.

> ***"The biggest challenge you face isn't the attacker. It's overcoming your own way of thinking in order to deal effectively with the attacker. And to be able to do it before he is successful."***
>
> **- Marc "Animal" MacYoung**

Let's Get Started With A Story

I first told the story about the big fight John and I engaged in with the two huge tankers in the bar outside Camp Casey, South Korea, in my book *Hard-Won Wisdom From the School of Hard Knocks:* , originally published by Paladin Press in 1996 (Now out in a Revised & Expanded edition).

More recently, I shared the story in *Campfire Tales from Hell: Musings on Martial Arts, Survival, Bouncing, and General Thug Stuff* edited by Rory Miller (2012). Besides the stories by Miller and me, this excellent anthology features lessons from Marc MacYoung, Wim Demeere, Lawrence Kane, Barry Eisler, and many others. It's a book I recommend. But let's get back to those two giants in South Korea. First I'll share what happened that night, and then I'll tell you the importance in regards to your fighter's mindset.

Tongduchon (TDC), South Korea

The two behemoths strutted in, pinging my radar immediately, and walked past tables and the dance floor to where they could order another drink. While the first in this bar, it was obvious the two had downed a number of drinks elsewhere before arriving at this club. I noticed the giant in the corner by the door also observing the pair. He was the only one in the bar bigger than these two, and from his vantage point, he didn't miss much. I shook my head as the two tried to be cool. One even had a pair of sunglasses on.

John and his girlfriend headed toward the dance floor, John motioning for me to follow. I reluctantly got up and did so. I was there to be the "fourth" since John's girlfriend had a friend visiting from Seoul.

Normally I preferred the smaller, quieter places that had pool tables rather than dance floors. I liked the little joints in Kwangamdong, just outside of Camp Hovey, but John liked the larger clubs outside Camp Casey in Tongduchon, or TDC as it was called by most GI's.

So, there I was, on a dance floor, feeling almost as uncomfortable as the Korean girl I was dancing with. She spoke very little English, and was obviously intimidated by the loud soldiers that filled the bar. But we were both being good friends by accompanying the two who were enjoying the place.

The pair of gorillas reappeared as they pushed their way through the crowd on the dance floor. They were intentionally bullying through, not even trying to be polite. As one walked behind the girl I was dancing with, he grabbed her behind. Not a mere brush, but an intentional grab that made her flinch away like a scared animal. I immediately stepped toward him and grabbed his wrist. Mr. Sunglasses had pushed the eyewear up into his hair line, so I was staring up into his eyes as I said, "You don't do shit like that."

Without a doubt, serving in the Armed Forces will help you develop a fighter's mindset.
(Picture courtesy of U.S. Department of Defense)

It must have been the paratrooper-sniper bravado that kept my voice steady, because as I looked up at this guy I started wondering just what I'd gotten myself into. He was huge! That was the last actual thought that I remember, because everything else came in a blur. I still had my hand grasping his left wrist that had grabbed my dance partner, stupidly thinking he'd back down and apologize, when his right hand reared back to throw an overhand right that most likely would have sent me into orbit if it had connected.

Now remember, we were still out on this crowded dance floor, so there was nowhere to move, let alone run. (As if running would have been in my paratrooper-sniper vocabulary.) I knew I didn't want to be hit by that humongous fist, so I just acted. I didn't think, I didn't plan, I didn't use any fancy martial art techniques. (While I'd studied various martial arts up to that time, I'd basically collected a variety of colored belts.)

Actually, I don't even remember exactly what I did. I do know this though. I attacked. I charged. I went forward with everything I had. I exploded into him with a flurry of knees, elbows and fists and found myself on the floor, on top of him, pounding on whatever I could pound. I do remember hammer-fisting his sunglasses into his head and smashing them. I remember hitting him with everything I had and thinking, "I can't give this guy a second chance."

Unbeknownst to me at the time, his buddy, equally huge, tried to join in the fight and pull me off of the guy I was pounding. John had stepped in and told the guy, "It's a one-on-one, stay out of it." The guy didn't listen, telling John what he could do, and went back for me. John stepped in and rearranged the guy's face with the class ring he was wearing.

While the fight started with me and the lumbering, ass-grabbing behemoth, by the time I stopped pounding and got to my feet, the entire bar had erupted into a massive brawl. It took me a couple minutes to find John and the girls. During that time, I don't remember everything, but I do remember the Korean bouncer of the place grabbed me, saying I started everything. I pushed, threw him to the floor, and continued looking. Someone grabbed me from behind and I turned swinging. At the last moment, I recognized that it was an American woman I was about to clobber, and I turned the hammer fist to the head into a push to the shoulder by opening my hand and lowering my swing.

When I reconnected with John, he was with the two girls who were both crying. As his girlfriend sobbed about the blood, he tried to reassure her by telling her it wasn't his. It wasn't working very well. People were still fighting and all we wanted was to get out of there before the Military Police, who were surely on their way, arrived.

I don't have anything against Military Police, but I will admit that I stayed in great shape so I could out run them if needed.

(Picture courtesy of U.S. Army)

We ushered the girls out the front door, and as we exited, the big guy in the corner, who hadn't moved, nodded his approval as I went by. We got into an alley and hid behind a couple of shrubs and bushes as a group of MPs ran past on the main sidewalk. When they went inside, we did some E&E (Escape and Evasion) back to John's girlfriend's hooch.

Once there, the girls stopped crying, but were not too talkative. John and I were still amped. While the ring he was wearing did a number on his opponent's face, it also broke his finger. I splinted it with a broken chopstick and an elastic hair band. It worked till he got to a medic the next day.

We found out later that the pair had been Tankers stationed at Camp Casey. Both had been taken to the hospital that night for stitches. The few in the bar that knew our names had kept their mouths shut. At least to the MPs.

When we got back to the barracks the next morning, the tale had been told. It probably grew a little here and there too, raising John's and my reputations as brawlers. There was a reason we called each other "squash partners" after the "squash" Clint Eastwood and William Smith played in *Any Which Way You Can*.

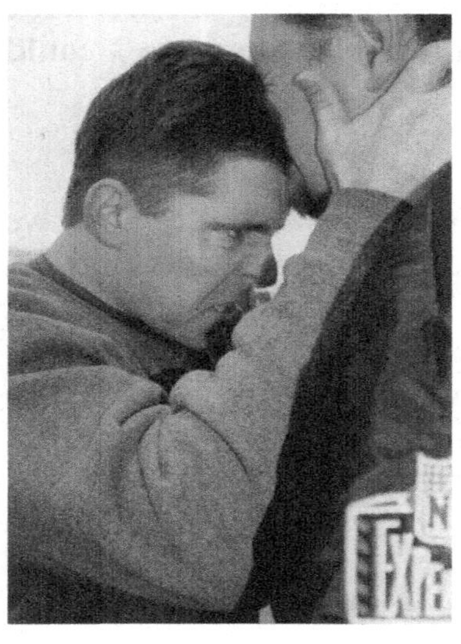

I've always been more of an infighter, and a solid head butt can be devastating when you are up close and personal.

- Alain Burrese

(Alain Burrese head butting a larger opponent.)

The two things I attribute to my success that night were my physical conditioning and the ability to go from zero to sixty in a heartbeat. When I was in the military, I considered maxing the PT (Physical Training) Test as a minimum standard. Strength and conditioning go a long ways in a physical encounter, especially against larger opponents.

Yes, I know about technique, but size and strength do matter. But most important that night was being able to launch immediately into my counterattack when he started to rear his arm back to pulverize my face. I do believe that if I'd have done anything else, he would have hit me, and that could have changed everything. While I've taken some good blows in my day, I can't say for certain what would have happened if he had connected. I don't think anyone can. I'm just grateful I didn't find out.

"Fighting is 90-percent mental and 10-percent technique. It's all about having a complete, or holistic, fight mentality."

- Kelly McCann

Many times, when violence happens, it erupts explosively with no time to think about what you are going to do. Sure, there are often many cues leading up to an attack, and through being aware, you can circumvent or prevent the altercation altogether. But other times it all happens blindingly fast. In those instances, you must be able to go from a dead stop to full speed without thought, without hesitation, and with full commitment. Anything less might not get the job done, and in these situations you cannot afford to fail.

If you want to protect yourself, you must first develop your fighter's mindset. This guide will show you the way.

Be Aware
Situational Awareness

"By learning to observe your environment, constantly evaluate it, and react appropriately to what you see, you can achieve a large degree of control over your fate."

- Tom Givens

You hear many self-defense instructors discussing situational awareness. It's a common term used in regard to both personal security and military operations. However, often it is used without defining what it actually means. I highly respect Kelly McCann, aka Jim Grover, for both his Combatives and Firearms instruction. His direct, no-nonsense, hard-hitting approach to self-defense is devastatingly effective. This is McCann's definition of situational awareness from his book *Combatives For Street Survival: Hard-Core Countermeasures for High-Risk Situations*: "Situational awareness is a cumulative alertness to threat and your environment. It enables you to notice pre-incident indicators, which are odd movements or anomalies given the situation. Cumulatively, pre-incident indicators create a visual unlikely circumstance consistent with either a contrived situation or predatorial behavior."

> ***"Comprehensive self-defense should begin with teaching a variety of awareness skills to help the student deal with a potential confrontation and prevent it from becoming violent."***
>
> **- Bill Kipp**

Awareness, or situational awareness, is the single best self-defense principle there is. Awareness enables you to avoid many violent encounters people face, and is the best way to ensure your safety. No matter what you know, how you train, or what weapons you carry, avoidance is the best way to prevent harm to yourself and loved ones. I put this principle of a fighter's mindset first because being aware is the foundation for any self-defense or safety program. It is the foundation of a fighter's mindset. If you pay attention to this information and incorporate being aware into your lifestyle, your chances to avoid a violent encounter increase. In addition, being aware allows you to attack back in those instances you can't de-escalate or avoid violence. (Not to mention, as I'll restate later, that you will also see a lot of good things out there that you might have otherwise missed.)

> ***"People should learn to see and so avoid all danger. Just as a wise man keeps away from mad dogs, so one should not make friends with evil men."***
>
> **- Buddha**

So let's explore this concept a bit more. When it comes to situational awareness, one of the first things I like to teach is a simple color code of awareness that was first made popular by Colonel Jeff Cooper, founder of the American Pistol Institute. Many self-defense instructors teach a variation of this code, and it can be a useful tool to help think about your fighter's mindset and a reminder that you need to be alert to indicators that will tip you off that something is amiss. Once we have the color code framework, we can better understand how we can be more aware and what to look for.

Four Levels of Awareness: White, Yellow, Orange and Red

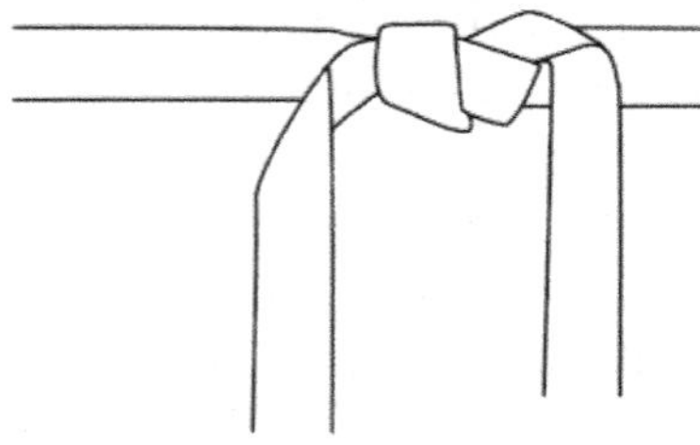

Level 1: White. This is the first level, and unfortunately the level where most people exist. In white, you are oblivious to your surroundings and unaware of any potential threats. In this state, you are not prepared mentally or physically to attack back if confronted with a violent or life-threatening encounter. Nor are you ready to flee if that is the best course of action. (And often it is.) With cell phones and other electronic devices, it seems that more and

more people walk around in the white level of awareness. Some places have actually passed laws making it a misdemeanor to cross a street while using an electronic device. Why? Because people were getting hit by cars while texting or talking on cell phones as they walked out into traffic. Do we really need the government telling us to quit texting and pay attention when you cross the street? Didn't our mothers and fathers teach us that as kids? The only times you should be in white are when you are secure in a locked safe place. For example, you can let your guard down, relax, and veg out when at home with all the doors locked. Otherwise, I recommend you stay at level 2, or yellow, the majority of the time.

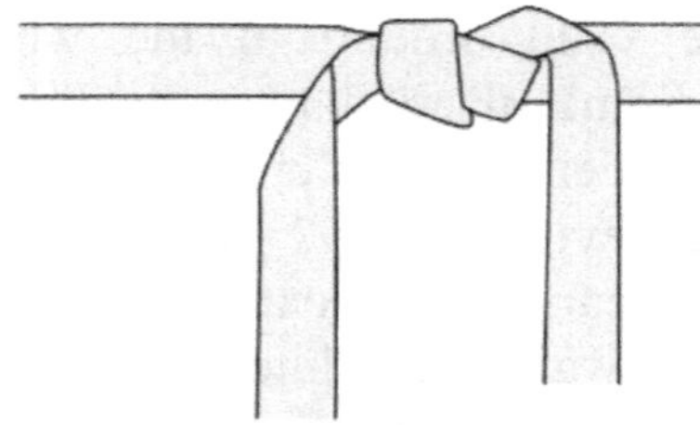

Level 2: Yellow. This is the level you should live in. My friend Ray Terry, a martial arts and firearms instructor, always likes to say, "Yellow is a great place to live." Condition yellow is having the mindset of paying attention and being aware of what is going on around you. You are aware of the general threats that surround you, such as being in a bad part of town, as well as noticing things or people that don't seem right. You are not paranoid. You are aware!

Besides living a much safer life by being in condition yellow and aware, you can live a fuller life by noticing the good things surrounding you, that otherwise go unnoticed as you blindly go along in condition white, oblivious to your surroundings. Besides noticing potential or actual threats, you also notice the new store that just opened across the street, the five dollar bill blowing across the sidewalk, or numerous other positive things you would miss if you were not paying attention to your surroundings. This is important, you notice everything: good, potentially bad, and bad. But it is NOT being paranoid, looking for danger around every corner. It is just being aware of your surroundings.

Unfortunately, the way some people teach situational awareness, it's at a level that becomes hard to maintain, especially for civilians. It becomes difficult to always be scanning for danger, and you can burn out if you try to maintain such high levels of hyper-vigilant awareness. Not only is there the possibility of burn out, but there is also the possibility that you will overreact when you are constantly on high alert looking for that boogie-man threat out there around every corner. So chill out some. Be alert. Be aware. But don't turn into a paranoid, hyper-vigilant, super-duper, ninja-commando, looking for deadly threats around every corner, under every rock, and behind every bush and tree. Remember, being aware lets you notice that beautiful sunset too. So be sure to take a moment to enjoy it.

> ***"The best self-defense is being aware of and avoiding dangerous people and hazardous situations."***
>
> **- Lawrence A. Kane & Kris Wilder**

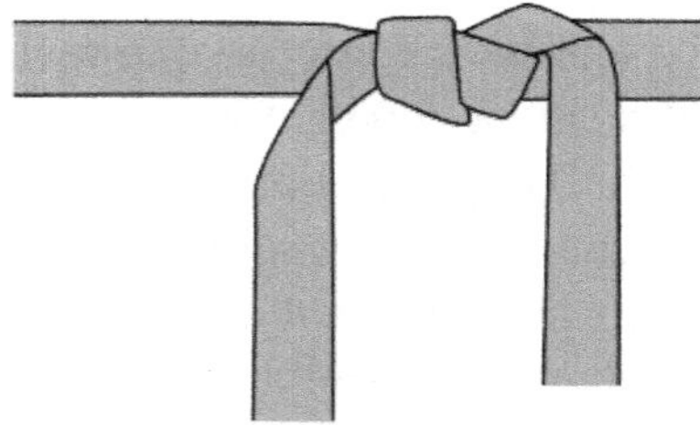

Level 3: Orange. This is the level when you notice a specific threat. Your perception of your surroundings must be more acute, because you have recognized some danger. You don't get trapped in tunnel vision and only focus on the threat, but because of the heightened sense of danger, you are more aware of everything around you. You look for avenues of escape, potential weapons, and other people that may help you. You also look for other people or things associated with your potential threat.

This heightened awareness at level orange is where you could burn out if kept up too long. You don't want to stay at this level all the time. It's only when you are generally aware and paying attention in yellow, and you recognize something that needs extra attention, or action, that you raise your awareness level to orange. When the situation is over you drop back down to your general yellow level of paying attention.

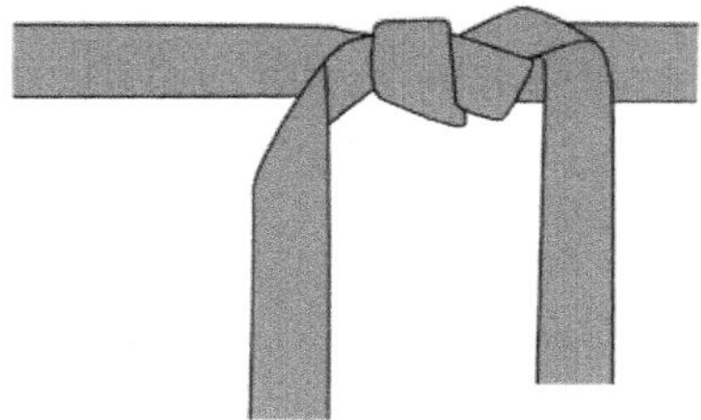

Level 4: Red. This is the level where it is time to act. You must escape or attack back. This is when the punks on the corner that were eying you start to advance quickly drawing weapons, or when the drunk that has been talking trash grabs a bottle and swings at your head, or when the car door opens after the car had been slowly creeping up the street toward you walking on the sidewalk.

Please remember, you won't necessarily be walking around telling yourself, "Stay in awareness level yellow. Oh look, he looks scary, go to level orange. Oh no, he's attacking, I must go to level red and run away or attack back."

The colors let us conceptualize these mental states and make them easier to discuss and understand. Hopefully they make them a bit easier to remember too. The key is to learn to go up and down through the levels as situations dictate. Your surroundings will constantly change, and you must be able to change your awareness level appropriately with these changes as you go through your daily routines.

"To see the sun and moon is no sign of sharp sight; to hear the noise of thunder is no sign of a quick ear."

- Sun Tzu

In all of these situations, your being at level 2, yellow, should have given you advance warning that something was not right, and when you noticed that, you raised your level to 3, orange, paying even closer attention to what was happening. Then, upon realizing there is an actual threat and violence is about to happen, you are prepared to react instantly to flee, defend, or attack back. The important element is being able to transition rapidly from yellow, to orange, to red. Sometimes, this transition is so fast that level orange is but a second; you must react instantly upon the first hint of a threat.

"She said she was meeting her boyfriend in Key West and wanted to be ready for the visit."

- Trooper Gary Dunick, describing what Ms. Barnes was thinking after she got into an accident while shaving her bikini area while driving.

Most people have an increased sense of awareness when driving. It's a must to prevent accidents. You should be driving in condition yellow. (Don't get me started on texting and other things while driving. Hear about the woman shaving her bikini area while driving? Look it up on google. In one report, the highway patrol officer that pulled her over said it was one of his stranger traffic stops.)

So, when you see a deer on the side of the road, or a child playing in an urban setting, or any other potentially dangerous situation that is not normal, you pay more attention, possibly taking your foot off the gas, watching the object of concern more closely in case the deer or child decides to bound into the road or create some other danger. If a deer or child does bound into the road, you immediately go from condition orange, where you were watching closer, to red, where you hit the brakes or take evasive action.

Seeing deer in the road does you no good if you don't know that hitting the brakes will stop the car from hitting them.

Part of awareness is being aware of what response you must do. Seeing the deer enter the road does you no good if you don't know that hitting the brakes will stop the car from hitting them. (And yes, I know you can do everything right and still hit a deer, but by being aware it reduces the likelihood of hitting one; it doesn't eliminate it. And that is the same with any self-defense situation. We try to reduce, because you can't eliminate everything.)

These are examples of how you may go through the conditions of awareness to keep yourself from harm while driving. Unfortunately, many people drift off into condition white, oblivious to what's going on while driving and accidents occur. Paying attention to the cell phone, radio, or food you dropped instead of the road can mean disaster. Not paying attention when a criminal is sizing you up as a target can mean disaster of another kind.

Driving is probably what helped me learn to be more aware and observant. Here in Montana we see lots of animals beside, and in, the road. When I was a kid, my dad always saw game before anyone else in the car, and he was driving. I learned from him and got good at it too. (I'm sure that, shooting, and other field craft he taught me in the woods helped with the military later.)

I remember when I and a group of Honor's College students drove a University van down to Flagstaff, AZ for an Honor's conference. We were down in the lower part of Utah, heading south, and Deb was driving. I was in the passenger seat. Others were sleeping in the back seats. I kept saying, "Deer." I was always seeing them before she did, and she was driving. (Not good.)

She finally asked me to drive. Fortunately, we switched. She fell asleep, and I was the only one awake as I drove. I saw the deer off the side, took my foot off the gas. They all decided to run across the road. I hit the brakes. Deb woke, saw all the deer in the road in front of us and screamed. The combination of her scream and falling off the seats as I hit the brakes woke everyone else up. I didn't hit any deer, and we continued our trip. Deb moved to the back to sleep while Matt came up front and stayed awake with me. We saw more deer, but none of them in the middle of the road. So this is what I'm talking about when I say be alert and be aware.

The key is to recognize the level you are at and be more aware, and then increase awareness to be prepared to act if needed. Make sure you live in the aware state and not in the oblivious state many people blunder around in. I want you aware, so you can recognize potential threats and enjoy the positive things out there. When you recognize a potential threat, increase your attention and attempt to avoid a violent encounter. If things get where you have to act, I want your awareness to have readied you for flight or fight. First try to escape or de-escalate, but if you have to, attack back. Being aware is the first step, and living in the level yellow is the key.

> ***"Escape or run to safety."***
>
> **- Michael Johnson**

I also want you to remember some advice from a friend of mine, Michael Johnson, a JKD instructor and fight choreographer for the stage. Rather than teaching people to run from danger, he teaches, "Escape or run toward safety." When you run, you should run toward safety.

An easy example would be in a mall parking lot, a common place for certain crimes. Run back toward the mall, where there are people, security guards, and safety. Running to your vehicle parked out on the fringes with no one around may not provide much protection from your attackers, especially if they can get to you before you can unlock the door, get in, and take off. All of which will take longer than you might think. Your awareness and staying in level yellow will enable you to know where safety lies if you have to run from some threat. So remember, don't just run from danger, run toward safety.

What Are You Looking For?

Awareness alone is not sufficient. You must act on the information you receive from your observations. It also helps to know what to look for. Sure, I can tell you to be aware, but aware of what? What are you looking for? What signs should you look for and then react to?

> ***"Realize that crime is a process. Not only that, but once you know what it looks like, it is very obvious when it is developing. The problem is that often we are so emotionally involved, that we fail to recognize the signs."***
>
> **- Marc "Animal" MacYoung**

Here's a simple example of awareness from living in Montana. When I'm out in the woods I'll notice and observe the different wildlife the Big Sky Country has in abundance. However, it is not enough to just observe wild animals. I must recognize each animal. My actions are quite different when encountering a bear on the trail than they are with a 6 point buck.

I want to take pictures of both, but my actions are different because of the threat differences. If it happened to be a grizzly, then my precautionary actions would increase more. You need to be aware, but you also need to recognize the different threats so that you can react accordingly. While most of us know the difference in danger levels between a grizzly and a deer, many don't recognize the danger signs human predators give. The better we recognize and react to criminals and those that would do us harm, the safer we will be.

Obviously I can't disclose every little thing you may notice that leads to violence, but I can point out some common things to look for that will raise your awareness level and help you avoid violence that may follow.

> ***"Here are some universal pre-incident indicators of imminent street crime or pending violent assault: No cover for action, no cover for status; Sudden change in someone's status; Correlation of movement; Hidden hands that cause unnatural movement."***
>
> **- Kelly McCann**

In no real particular order, here are a few examples that should cause you to go from level yellow to orange. You might recognize someone moving with purposeful movements towards or away from you that doesn't seem normal. Maybe it is convergent movement you notice. It may be seeing something, a car or person, more than once because they are following you. Perhaps it is a slow moving car or person, with someone "scoping" you or the surroundings. Pay attention to something that is there that should not be there. Pay attention when something changes at a coincidental time.

Look around and notice if someone is loitering in the parking lot or garage. If they are, maybe you should go back inside until it is safe. If you don't go back, at least pay more attention. Don't just focus on the first loiterers, they may be there to draw your attention away from the real threat coming up behind you. Remember to pay attention to everything. Now, think of things that would require you to pay a little closer attention. Thinking of them beforehand will increase your ability to recognize them when it really counts.

> ***Unfortunately, tunnel vision is a physiological effect of imminent danger, making it more difficult to pay attention to everything.***

You should increase your awareness entering dark areas, or places where you have to transition to something, such as unlocking a car or opening a door. Any time your attention may be distracted with something such as fumbling for keys, looking for a key hole, etc. you should be aware. It is at these times that criminals like to attack, since they can often surprise you when your attention is on something else. For this reason, you want to ensure that you are being aware of your surroundings and increase your awareness for certain circumstances.

Known trouble areas often warrant an increase in attentiveness, as do certain enclosed areas like elevators. So know the territory or neighborhood you are in. Are you in an area with gang activity? Can you spot gang members? Find out about the local culture where you are. This is especially important if you travel to different countries. Think of some areas where you want to have a heightened sense of awareness.

In addition to keeping yourself safe, being aware may help you thwart other criminal or terrorist activities. It goes without saying since 9/11 people became more aware of the possibilities of terrorist acts and realize law enforcement officers can't do it all. We can help keep our nation safer by being more aware. If we see certain patterns of behavior, we can report to the authorities and help stop those who want to commit crimes of terror.

Things to look out for and report include: suspicious packages, luggage, or mail abandoned in crowded places; someone suspiciously exiting a secured, non-public area near a train or bus depot, airport, tunnel, bridge, government building, or tourist attraction; someone suspiciously watching, mapping or photographing a landmark, airport, tunnel, bridge government building, business, or tourist attraction; and things such as strange odors, smoke, fire or explosions.

> ***"Your new attitude should include an awareness of where you are and what's going on around you. It's like when you're driving: you check the rearview mirror, watch for flashing brake lights up ahead,***

quickly rehearse the turns you'll be making… all at once."

- Stanford Strong

To recognize suspicious behavior, you must first be aware, and second know what behavior should be observed. Unlike the criminal that wants to attack you, terrorists usually are looking at different targets, those that create the biggest impact for their time and effort. To pull these acts off, it takes planning. You may be able to spot this planning if you keep your eyes and ears open for these signs or behaviors. Unfortunately, unless you have been in certain military or law enforcement fields, you probably have not been exposed to the kinds of behaviors to observe.

My father taught me of the importance to watch others when I was young. When he was in Vietnam, and they would catch someone pacing out distances, it was a sign that someone was up to no good. Spies would measure distances from fences to buildings, or from building to building, to provide to the opposing side. Warning signs today could be someone pacing a distance, sketching a picture of a place, video taping the lights and surveillance cameras rather than normal things a person would video. A person might also check out fences, peak periods, escape routes and other particulars of a potential target. Take note of things such as unattended packages, suspicious vehicle activity, and any individuals whose activities and actions do not seem normal in the sense of peaceful or harmlessly motivated.

Noticing just one of these is probably no big deal, but if someone is linked to several of these actions and appears to be suspicious and not normal, you may wish to notify authorities. When doing so, articulate what you saw as detailed as you can. Don't get excited and paranoid, but if you notice something out of the ordinary, report it, and then go about your business. Don't try and be a cop or soldier unless you are one. Just like your personal safety is your responsibility, our nation's safety is our responsibility, and by being aware, we can help do our part.

Become a Keen Observer

Have you ever played the game where you close your eyes and try to mentally describe to a friend, your surrounding environment? Try it. It's not as easy as it sounds, especially if you don't know it is coming. If you know you are going to be tested, you will pay more attention. Most of the time, if we were stopped suddenly and asked to do this, we would not fare as well as we believe we would. Even when we think we are aware, we are probably observing a lot less than we believe.

To increase your awareness, you need to practice being a keen observer. You need to pay more attention to your surroundings. I've found it easy to play mental games with myself to help observe more. You can also do this with a friend. As you are walking, pay attention to things and then mentally quiz yourself, or if with a friend, quiz each other on things you have passed.

Do this often, and you begin to notice more on a regular basis. I was lucky growing up in the country. I can remember driving with my father who would always spot various animals. He'd say, "See the deer," and my sister and I would peer out the windows looking for what he spotted. With practice, and over time, I learned to spot these animals quickly too. This skill that enabled us to see the various wildlife in the fields and woods, has also enabled me to recognize potentially dangerous situations in other circumstances. Practicing looking for anything can aid you in becoming more aware.

KIMS = Keep-In-Memory-System

In sniper school, we used to play the KIMS game. KIMS stands for Keep-In-Memory-System. The instructors would select six to twelve ordinary items, such as a pen, fired cartridge, stapler, etc., and place them under a blanket. The students would then gather around the blanket, and it would be removed for one to two minutes. The students could not pick up the items but could move, so they could see easier or from a different view. No note taking was allowed.

Any assortment of items can be used for the KIMS game.

When time was up, each student had a test and had to write down at least five categories regarding each object. 1. What it appeared to be: (a stapler). 2. Its shape: (draw a sketch of the stapler). 3. Its dimensions: (6 inches long, 2 inches high, 1 ½ inches wide). 4. Its color: (gray). 5. Its condition: (New, worn, etc.). If you didn't have all five areas for an item, you did not get credit for that item. To make the exercise more difficult, more items would be displayed with less viewing time, and then less time to recall and write down the five categories. To make it even more challenging, after viewing the items, the students would have to undergo some form of activity or physical training and then return to the class room and remember the items viewed earlier. You can take this idea and create your own games to help your awareness levels. If you have kids, it's a great game to teach them to pay closer attention to things and to improve memory and recall.

Pretend You are a Criminal

Another good exercise to help increase your awareness is to pretend you are a criminal. Earlier, I asked you to think about things that would make you increase your awareness, and then asked what kinds of places would require a heightened awareness level. Now I want you to think like a criminal for a bit.

Where would you hide to rob someone at the ATMs you visit?

As you go to an ATM, ask yourself where you would hide or what avenue of approach you would use to rob someone there. Sit in the mall for a while and watch people. Which people would be easier to rob? Which people would be more difficult? Why? This last question can be hard to answer. You may find yourself saying, "I don't know. That person just looks easier." Analyze why you have those feelings and thoughts. The more you practice, the more aware you will become, and the better you will be at spotting things and understanding what you are observing.

Paying attention takes both physical and mental energy. You will get tired trying to observe every little thing. But with practice and repetition, like other exercise, it becomes easier and less tiring. The benefits of being a keen observer are well worth the time and practice. Besides noticing things that enrich your life, keen observation just may save it.

Be Aware of Yourself

So far, everything regarding awareness has been targeted toward paying attention to what is going on around you, and what to look for to help ensure your safety. It's extremely important to pay attention and be aware of external things, but you must also be aware of yourself. You must be aware of your strengths, weaknesses, and limitations, as well as how you effect your environment.

First, take a good assessment of your strengths and weaknesses regarding self-defense and attacking back. Are you in great shape? Are you in terrible shape? Do you have physical limitations? Do you have martial art training? Have you trained with weapons before? What kind of lifestyle do you lead? Do you go out partying a lot, or do you stay home with the family?

Take a real close look at yourself: physically, mentally, emotionally, your habits and your lifestyle. I'm not going to tell you what life to lead, just know yourself, and what you do, so that you can prepare accordingly. If you are in better shape with no physical limitations, you will have a better chance at being able to attack back. Additionally, you may not be a primary target for the criminal looking for an easy score.

If you look like someone who will fight back, the criminal may just go somewhere else. If you party a lot in places where violence occurs, know this and take extra precautions. Go with friends, limit your alcohol consumption, and stay extra alert. There are no absolutes, but knowing yourself will help you make decisions and be better prepared.

Second, be aware of how your actions effect a situation. Your actions can antagonize or diffuse; they can escalate or de-escalate; they can assist you in going home safely, or result in you having to attack back for your life - and possibly losing. Acting like a jerk or being obnoxious and aggressive can lead to violence.

Being polite and taking an assertive but non-aggressive position with obnoxious people can help de-escalate potentially violent situations. Being aware of how your actions are effecting the situation is as important as being aware of what's going on around you, and they go hand in hand.

A theoretical example I often use consists of the options available when going into a bar frequented by bikers. I can go in and get along just fine, or I can go in and start bad mouthing anyone who rides a Harley. Which is the most conducive to my health?

Obviously, this is extreme, and one would need to be suicidal to go into a bar filled with bikers badmouthing Harleys. People do things just as obvious all the time that get themselves into trouble and hurt. These actions are obvious to everyone but them. They wake up in the hospital wondering what happened, and a friend says, "Man, you should have kept your mouth shut."

Another example that is fairly common involves the type of person who gets loud or vicious with words when angered but doesn't expect the confrontation to go physical. This type of person will yell, call people names, and swear profusely when angered. It can be directed at anyone anytime the person is riled. Some people will cower away or avoid such behavior, while others may take it to the next level and become physical.

Many people have been surprised when what they figured would be a loud argument got them punched in the mouth. Many men have been punched or worse for comments or looks directed at someone's girlfriend or wife. I could go on for several chapters about the stupidity I've seen, and the violence that erupted over such acts. Sometimes I was the one being stupid, and my actions and comments brought on violence that was definitely avoidable. Don't go there. You need to be aware of what you are doing and how it is affecting those around you. Do not provoke a situation that could have ended without violence. Paying attention to this, while paying attention to your surroundings, will keep you out of most trouble.

Avoid Being Prey

Criminals are predators, and like the predator in the wild, they prefer attacking weaker targets. By selecting the weak, they have a greater chance of success. Criminals don't want confrontation. They want an easy score. Confrontation raises risks for the predator as well, and it requires expending more energy, time, and resources. The predator and criminal want it over as quickly as possible, with him having the upper hand. (And they will often use surprise as an element to gain that upper hand.) He doesn't want to risk the possibility of injury, or of being identified. Therefore, make yourself stand out as someone who will not be an easy victim, and you will increase the odds the criminal predator will pass you by.

> ***"Learn from the experience of others and don't let yourself be surprised."***
>
> **- Colonel Jeff Cooper**

Just being aware, as I've already discussed, reduces the likelihood of you being an easy victim. Weak prey do not pay attention to their surroundings and don't realize the predator is there until too late. Your goal is not to stop the criminals. That is best left to the police. Your goal is to make it so you are not easy prey, so the criminal passes you by as a risk he doesn't want to take.

You need to recognize if you are giving off signals that may draw predators. Studies among criminals have shown they pick certain people as victims. If you are not exhibiting those characteristics, chances are you will not be selected as a weak target. You have probably heard these before, but they are worth repeating. You don't want to look like a victim, so you walk erect, look around (that awareness stuff again), walk with someone, don't appear lost or confused, don't be preoccupied, watch how you carry your valuables, stay in well-lit areas, walk purposefully, and so forth.

There are other things you can do to reduce the likelihood of becoming a target of a criminal. Some of these are lifestyle habits, and it is up to you how to live your life. Just be aware that what you do, how you behave, where you go, and how you dress can make a difference when being sized up by a predator. Expensive clothes and jewelry will be noticed and may invite trouble. Certain bars and areas of town are more frequented by criminals than others. Areas are different and frequented by different people at 2:00 A.M. than in the middle of the day.

I want you to think about these things. You probably have a good idea of what things invite attention - and what things don't. Most people have instincts that will help them, and I recommend you listen to yours. Way too often I hear people saying, "I had a feeling I shouldn't have done that," or "I had a feeling about that guy," or "I knew I shouldn't have done that or gone there." Failing to listen to your feelings and instincts can lead you to trouble. So remember, when those warning bells go off inside your head, LISTEN!

Take Care – Be Aware

Developing alertness and awareness skills is the most important ingredient to your personal safety. Without developing these skills, you will be at a tremendous disadvantage when it comes to protecting yourself and ultimately defending yourself if you can't avoid the threats and dangers that your awareness alerts you to. Being aware, or situational awareness, is the foundation of your fighter's mindset. No warrior can afford not to be aware of his or her surroundings and how he or she is interacting with and effecting those surroundings. So take care, be aware, and stay safe!

"Be aware. Be alert. Assess."

- Loren W. Christensen and Lisa Place

Lisa is not only aware of the threat Loren imposes, she is alert to the improvised weapon in her hand, and assesses it her best defense.

(Photo courtesy of Loren W. Christensen & Lisa Place)

Be Decisive

> ***"Direct threats require decisive action."***
>
> **- Dick Cheney**

When that behemoth grabbed me around the throat that night in Tongduchon, I had a split second to act. In such a situation, you have to take quick, decisive action in an instant. Any hesitation, or deliberation on what to do, can result in you getting seriously hurt.

I don't care who's throwing the punch, I'd rather not be on the receiving end of it.

Think about it. How long does it take to rear back your fist and send it flying into an opponent's face?

That is exactly what that huge tanker was doing. Albeit, the alcohol he drank that night might have slowed his actions down a little bit, but it still didn't take him long to rear that gorilla sized fist back to pulverize me, and it would have taken even less time to find its way from the cocked back position to the middle of my face.

In that short amount of time, I not only had to decide to act, I had to actually act and do something to prevent getting pulverized. My response to charge, tackle him to the ground, and pound on him with everything I had, might not have been the best response, but it was a response and it worked well for me at the time. And yes, I realize having John there to stop the other goon from stomping me when I was on the ground dealing with my giant was a blessing. But the fact is, I had to decide on something, and do it instantly. Decisiveness is part of the fighter's mindset.

To some degree, being decisive is a built in characteristic. It seems that some people must deliberate longer than others. However, in emergencies, and believe me, being attacked is an emergency, you don't have time to deliberate and weigh your options. You must be decisive and act immediately. The good news is you can increase your ability to be decisive. How much? That depends. But you can train to be more decisive than you are now, especially when it comes to defending and protecting yourself. This is the element of decisiveness that you must develop with your fighter's mindset.

Think about being faced with a violent physical assault, and it is evident that it will happen. (For whatever reason, your awareness, avoidance, and de-escalation skills failed.) Your physical well-being, and quite possibly your life, depends on your selecting a proper course of action and acting upon it without hesitation. And remember, sometimes the proper course of action might not be the "best" course of action, but it is good enough to see you through.

> ***"A good plan executed today is better than a perfect plan executed at some indefinite point in the future."***
>
> **- General George S. Patton, Jr.**

When someone attacks you, there is no time to dilly-dally. And as General Patton said, the specific course of action you decide upon is, within certain parameters, less important than doing something. You must decide, and you must act, NOW!

> ***"To ponder is quite possibly to perish."***
>
> **- Colonel Jeff Cooper**

I'm telling you to be decisive, and telling you to act upon your decision, but not really telling you what to decide. Obviously, like just about everything dealing with fighting and violence, it depends. However, most often, if you can't sprint away and escape, the proper course of action involves a strong counterattack. This is the premise of my book *Attack Back*.

This too, goes back to an old saying, "The best defense is a good offense." And while this is not 100% true, and I strongly believe a person must develop some good defensive skills to protect oneself, it does cover that you are not going to stop an attacker by defending.

You attack back with offensive measures with sufficient force and violence to prevent your attacker from inflicting serious injury or death to you, or your loved ones you are protecting. (This can also be true when protecting innocent third parties, if you decide to.) Again, there is that decisiveness trait as a major part of the fighter's mindset. Just as it wouldn't take an attacker long to hurt you, you only have a moment to decide to intervene and help someone else who is being beaten by a criminal attacker.

A person can be seriously injured or killed in a matter of seconds, so you don't have time to ponder what you should do. I strongly advise you to think about these things now, before you are ever faced with such a decision. Determine what situations you will get involved with, and how you might do so, and then it will be easier to decide and act when facing an emergency.

Obviously, this decision will be based on your level of confidence in your training and abilities. While everyone must attack back with everything they have when personally assaulted, only those of us with more training and skills may choose to get involved to protect others. You have to determine what you will do based on your own skills, level of training, and moral compass. I'm just telling you to think about it now, before you ever have to make such a decision, to make it easier to be decisive if the time ever comes.

"He who hesitates, meditates in a horizontal position."

- Grandmaster Ed Parker

The bottom line is when you are attacked, you must evaluate the situation and decide instantly on a proper course of action, and then act immediately with everything you have. To cultivate your fighter's mindset, you must be decisive.

The OODA Loop

It is difficult to discuss decisiveness without mentioning military strategist Colonel John Boyd (USAF) and the OODA Loop (sometimes referred to as Boyd's law). This concept states that one must Observe his opponent, Orient himself to his opponent and the unfolding events, Decide on a course of action based on that orientation as well as on his training and experience, and finally, Act out his decision.

If two combatants face off, the one who Moves through this loop faster will be provided a remarkable advantage over his opponent. It will allow the fighter to disrupt his opponent's ability to respond in a timely or effective manner. But what this also shows is that an aggressive attacker who initiates the action having already gone through the observation, orientation, and decision stages will have an overwhelming advantage over a reactive defender. This is why it can be suicidal to wait for the other guy to act first when you have a chance to do something right away.

John R. Boyd
Colonel, United States Air Force
(Picture courtesy of Arlington National Cemetery)

What this means to you is don't forget your situational awareness and train. Your training, practice, and drills, combined with good situational awareness, can help you move through the OODA loop faster. The more training and experience you have, the faster you can move through the cycle. Additionally, not only can a possible confrontation be avoided through being aware, it can allow you to observe, orient, decide and act much faster.

Be Courageous

"A healthy-minded boy should feel hearty contempt for the coward and even more hearty indignation for the boy who bullies girls or small boys, or tortures animals."

- Theodore Roosevelt

I was first going to name this section "Be Fearless." However, I don't think you can really eliminate fear, nor do I believe we really want to. Fear is natural, and if used, it can help save our hide in dangerous situations. It is when fear paralyzes people and prevents them from acting that it is bad. I believe that is the cowardice that President Roosevelt felt contempt for. (I'm not talking about the natural "freeze" response that can happen to people, but rather uncontrolled fear that prevents people from doing what they need to do.)

Therefore, I prefer the term Courageous, which is defined as "the quality of mind or spirit that enables a person to face difficulty, danger, pain, etc., without fear; bravery." When you are scared, but you do it anyway, that is courageous, and that is the fighter's mindset that I'm talking about. Feel the fear, but do it anyway.

"No passion so effectively robs the mind of all its powers of acting and reasoning as fear."

- Edmund Burke

Fear is natural, and a topic that needs to be studied by anyone practicing military or martial arts, engaging in military or police operations, or wanting to develop the fighter's mindset of being courageous. Courage requires feeling, confronting, and overcoming fear. Here are a few words on fear from two of our military's greatest Generals of WWII.

"If bravery is a quality which knows no fear, than I have never seen a brave man."

- General Douglas MacArthur

"And every man is scared in his first action. If he says he's not, he's a goddamn liar."

- General George S. Patton, Jr.

**Lt. General George S. Patton, Jr.
(Before his promotion to General)**

"The real hero is the man who fights even though he's scared. Some get over their fright in a minute, under fire; others take an hour; for some it takes days…"

- General George S. Patton, Jr.

When it comes to General Patton, I don't mind quoting him more than once in a row. He was a genius for war, and my favorite General to read about and study. If you read my works, you're going to see Patton quotes and lessons thrown in, sometimes generously.

Since fear is natural, and always present in combat, we must learn to control it. That is what being courageous is all about. I really like the title of one of Bill Kipp's books: *Turing Fear Into Power.* That is the goal of being courageous. Kipp's book is also an excellent guide on how adrenal stress response training can help turn fear from an enemy to a powerful ally.

Simulation or reality-based scenario training and tactical performance imagery are also excellent approaches to gaining experience and working toward being able to control fear. There are also psychological skills that can be practiced to further develop control for self-regulation of emotions such as fear and others. For further information on these, I strongly recommend the book *Warrior Mindset: Mental Toughness Skills for a Nation's Peacekeepers* by Michael J. Asken, Ph.D., Lt. Col. Dave Grossman, and Loren W. Christensen.

To attack back, you must overcome fear and be courageous. I agree with Colonel Cooper when he said, "Violent crime is feasible only if its victims are cowards. A victim who fights back makes the whole business impractical." Yes, you may get hurt fighting back, but what will happen if you don't fight back? If you fight back, you retain your dignity and self-respect and increase your chances of surviving.

(Later you'll read that I disagree vehemently with the old advice of not fighting your attacker. That old advice is plain wrong!) Fight back, regardless of any fear you are feeling. You'll be afraid, but be courageous and don't submit to acts of violence against you.

> ***"In war there is no substitute for victory, and this is equally true of personal combat, which is, after all, a microcosm of war. When a coward is offered deadly violence, his reaction may be to surrender, or cower, or flee, or call for help; not one of these choices is likely to obviate his peril."***
>
> **- Colonel Jeff Cooper**

Fear, and the adrenaline surge that comes with it, can be used to your advantage when controlled. You can be faster, stronger, tougher and more resilient with adrenaline pumping through your body. However, while it can help you survive, it also robs you of fine motor skills and higher thought processes. So part of being courageous is keeping things simple and straightforward in order to be effective. Techniques that don't require fine motor skills or complex thoughts are easier to perform under adrenalized stress, and therefore enable you to act. Acting, despite of fear, is courage.

The famous story of the tea master and the *ronin* illustrates the proper martial mindset of no fear (being courageous) and total concentration on the moment. I've read the story in several places, but I'm including the version found in *Surviving Armed Assaults: A Martial Artist's Guide To Weapons, Street Violence, & Countervailing Force* by Lawrence A. Kane. Lawrence is a friend of mine, and I strongly encourage you to read *Surviving Armed Assaults*, and the others he's authored or co-authored, especially those found in the further reading section of this book. I've also included a couple of Lawrence's comments from before and after the story.

Begin *Surviving Armed Assaults* excerpt:

There is a concept called the fearlessness of no fear. It is about the quintessential martial mindset, total concentration on the moment. The famous story of the tea master and the *ronin* sheds some interesting insight into this concept:

At the insistence of Lord Yamanouchi the *daimyo* of Tosa Province, a reluctant tea master was taken to Yedo (Yedo is the feudal name for the modern city of Tokyo.) on an official trip attired in *samurai* garb, including the two traditional swords of the warrior class. While running an errand for his master in the city, the tea master was accosted by a *ronin* (A *ronin* is a masterless *samurai*, literally a wave man (one who is tossed about like the waves on the sea). Lacking a benefactor, many *ronin* took up criminal endeavors to support themselves.). Since he was by himself and dressed beyond his station, this was exactly the thing the tea master feared might happen.

At first, he was so scared that he was unable to speak, yet was finally able to admit that he was not really a *samurai*. Upon discovering that his opponent was merely a tea master and not a fearsome warrior, the *ronin* was more determined than ever to take his money. The *ronin* declared that it would be an insult to the tea master's province if he did not defend his honor. The tea master replied, "If you so insist, we will try out our skills, but first I must finish my master's errand. Then I will return tomorrow morning for a duel."

The *ronin* agreed and the tea master rushed to complete his errand so that he could talk with the master of a local *dojo* before his fateful meeting with the *ronin*. He intended to ask the sword master how he might die in the manner befitting a *samurai*. The sword master was taken aback by the question, saying, "You are unique. Most students come ask me how to use a sword. You come to me asking how to die. Before I teach you the art of dying, please serve me a cup of tea."

Forgetting about his impending catastrophe, the tea master prepared tea in the manner he always did—as if there were nothing else in the world that mattered except for serving the tea. Deeply moved by the tea master's intense, but natural concentration, the sword master exclaimed, "That's it! That very state of mind is what you will need tomorrow when you go to meet the *ronin*. First think of serving tea to an honored guest and act accordingly. Draw your sword and close your eyes. When you hear his *kiai* (spirit shout), strike him with your sword. The contest will probably end with a mutual slaying."

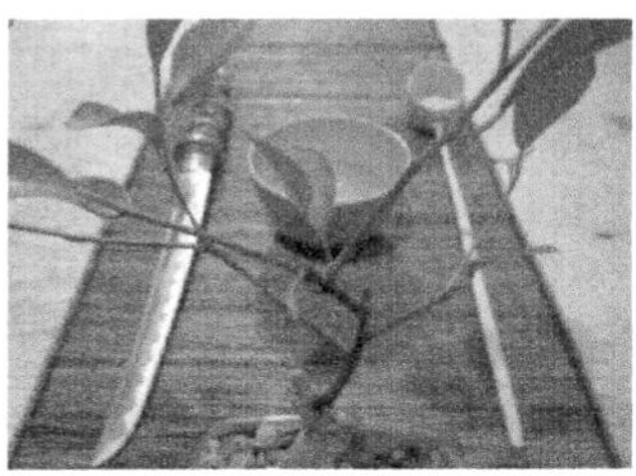

The tea master thanked the sword master and went on about his business. The next morning when he went to meet the *ronin*, he followed the sword master's advice to the letter. The tea master boldly stood before his opponent, the embodiment of concentration. The *ronin*, who had previously seen a coward, now faced the personification of bravery. Instead of advancing to attack, the *ronin* retreated. Cowed with fear inspired by the superior concentration of his adversary, he turned and fled. After standing a while and hearing no shout, the tea master opened his eyes to gaze upon an empty street.

This is an example of what the Japanese call *fudoshin* or indomitable spirit. Miyamoto Musashi, arguably the greatest swordsman who ever lived, demonstrated the ultimate evolution of such spirit. In his writings, he related that many opponents fell before his sword simply because they believed that they would, not necessarily, because he was the better warrior.

When your life is on the line, fight not only for yourself but also about those who care about and depend upon you—your children, your spouse, your family, and your friends. In the heat of battle you will not have time to think of anything beyond the immediate but it is wise to consider beforehand what will happen to your loved ones if you do not make it. Sometimes the impact to others can be even more motivating than the impact to yourself. You must make a wholehearted commitment to survive.

End *Surviving Armed Assaults* excerpt.

I think it is also important to recognize that having the fighter's mindset of being courageous is not only a trait that will enable you to be prepared to protect or defend yourself, but one that allows you to live life at its fullest.

> ***"Life shrinks or expands in proportion to one's courage."***
>
> **- Paul Martinelli**

So be courageous and live your life as a warrior. Don't let fear keep you from pursuing your dreams and living a life full of adventure. It's important to be prepared for potential emergencies and to be able to defend yourself. However, it is more important to live a life without fear and full of rich experiences.

So be courageous and don't let fear hold you back from your dreams ever again.

I want to end this section with one of my favorite quotes on courage. It's another from President Theodore Roosevelt, and I feel it's fitting that I started and ended this section with him. I'm sure you've read it before, but it never hurts to remind yourself again.

> ***"It is not the critic who counts: not the man who points out how the strong man stumbles or where the doer of deeds could have done better. The credit belongs to the man who is actually in the arena, whose face is marred by dust and sweat and blood, who strives valiantly, who errs and comes up short again and again, because there is no effort without error or shortcoming, but who knows the great enthusiasms, the great devotions, who spends himself for a worthy cause; who, at the best, knows, in the end, the triumph of high achievement, and who, at the worst, if he fails, at least he fails while daring greatly, so that his place shall never be with those cold***

and timid souls who knew neither victory nor defeat."

- Theodore Roosevelt

Rough Rider Colonel Roosevelt

(Picture courtesy of the Theodore Roosevelt Association)

Be Willing

When I was with the 2nd Infantry Division in South Korea, my "squash" buddy, John, and I had letterman type jackets made. I called it my sniper jacket due to having different sniper and unit identifiers sewn on it. On the front, I had a ranger scroll located on the upper left side. This scroll had my units from the 82nd Airborne Division and 2nd Infantry Division on the ends. (3/505 and 1/503 for those who care about such things.) In the main part of the scroll, I had: "It's Not The Skill To Win – It's The Will To Win." This is such an important part of a fighter's mindset. You must not only have the will to win, but also the will to hurt, and even kill, an attacker that is trying to do the same to you.

Most people are decent, law-abiding, citizens who never think about hurting others. Not only don't they think about it, they have a horror of inflicting harm to fellow human beings and often loath those who do. For these people, most people, it is extremely difficult to accept that they might have to actually hurt or kill someone to save themselves or loved ones. And if it is difficult to accept, it is even more difficult to actually do something that hurts or kills another human being. Yes, even if it is to save themselves or others. Therefore, it is extremely important that one develop the will to do whatever it takes to protect oneself when developing the fighter's mindset.

"You must understand that for a civilized normal human being, the taking of a fellowman's life is an unnatural act."

- Massad Ayoob

Often, when I'm talking to groups of women, they become a bit squeamish when I talk about things such as gouging eyeballs, crushing the throat, stabbing pens into ears and eyes, and so forth. (Actually, some become very squeamish.) But these are things that a smaller female can do to stop a larger male from raping or killing her. And believe it or not, some women just can't think of themselves doing such things, even to save their own life. (Some men can't think of themselves doing such things either.)

What sometimes helps get them into the proper mindset of being willing to hurt or kill another human is when the women are also mothers. I have them imagine someone trying to hurt their child when their sons or daughters were babies. (Having them think about their babies works much better than thinking about teenagers.)

Most people would leave this mother grizzly alone. A human mother can be just as ferocious protecting her baby, and that is the fighter's mindset you must have.

Many people, especially women, would do anything to protect their babies, even more than they would to protect themselves. That is the feeling, the attitude, the mindset that we must develop as part of a fighter's mindset. The warrior will do whatever it takes, and that means having the "will" to do whatever it takes.

This goes for tough guys who talk a good game too. I've seen more than one person talk like they had the will, but when the feces hit the oscillating blades, it was a whole different story. Real violence is scary and actually hurting or killing someone is not the same as in video games. It's also something you will have to live with for the rest of your life.

A friend of mine describes it as the "Cost of it." (This "Cost of it" can include nightmares, depression, social withdrawal, impotence, and alcoholism among the post-incident trauma that is part of the aftermath of having to seriously injure or kill someone in self-defense.) I remember my grandfather, who had a Silver Star and two Purple Hearts from WWII, tell me one time, "You don't forget getting shot. You don't forget shooting someone either." He didn't really talk much about his time in the war, but I know he made a couple beach landings in the Pacific. (While *Saving Private Ryan* was about the Normandy invasion, with the Omaha Beach assault at the beginning, the landings in the Pacific were very ugly too.) I still remember that comment he made that evening we were having dinner together.

We must never forget what those who served have done for us.

What are your moral beliefs? Do you believe that it is immoral to kill another human under any circumstances? Some do. I cannot tell you what is right. I can tell you that I personally believe it is okay to hurt or kill a person in defense of yourself or another, but you will have to decide that on your own, or maybe with your spiritual adviser.

Regardless of what you decide, you need to know. Knowing what you are willing to do is important in regards to your personal protection and self-defense strategies. Also note that if you believe like I do, that there are times when it is acceptable to hurt or kill others to save yourself or others, some people will believe you are immoral and speak against you. And that's okay by me, because I have similar feelings about them not protecting themselves or loved ones.

I want to briefly address a belief that prohibits some from having the will to kill another in defense of themselves, and that is the belief that the Ten Commandments found in the Bible say "Thou shalt not kill." Biblical scholars say that in the original Hebrew, the Sixth Commandment was, "Thou shalt not *murder*." Murder is the illegal killing of the innocent by criminals, and therefore the Ten Commandments don't prohibit you from killing in a justified self-defense situation. I encourage you to discuss this with your religious leader or spiritual advisor if you have concerns in regards to defending yourself and your spiritual beliefs.

If you have any inhibitions or beliefs against hurting or killing another human being in defense of yourself or others, you must find within yourself the will to do so if you want to fully develop the fighter's mindset. How you reconcile your willingness to hurt or kill another human being with your principles of being a good human and citizen will be up to you. It is a decision you will have to make, and one you will have to implement immediately in the event that your convictions are ever put to the test. (And I sincerely hope that through awareness and avoidance, they never are.)

When you have the will to win, the willingness to do whatever it takes to protect yourself or loved ones from harm, you can attack back with determination and the physical wherewithal to successfully defeat an aggressor set to physically harm you or others. Develop your fighter's mindset and be willing.

> ***"Controlled and properly channeled anger will afford you tremendous strength of courage, mind, and body. Anger blots out pain. Anger strengthens muscles and anger heightens mental alertness. Through anger you will be able to do things you never dreamed you could. Turn that anger against your attacker with immediate and explosive force. Unbalance him with your fury."***
>
> **- Lt. Jim Bullard**

Be Vicious

"Anyone who willfully and maliciously attacks another without sufficient cause deserves no consideration."

- Colonel Jeff Cooper

When your life is on the line, and there is risk of serious bodily injury or death to your person, you must attack back viciously to defeat your attacker and go home safe. When you have the will to defend yourself, and you've made the decision to do so, you must do everything necessary to save yourself. This often means you must be more vicious than your attacker.

You didn't initiate the violence. You tried to avoid or de-escalate it if possible. But when all else fails, and you must go physical to save yourself, you must counter-attack explosively with overwhelming violence of your own.

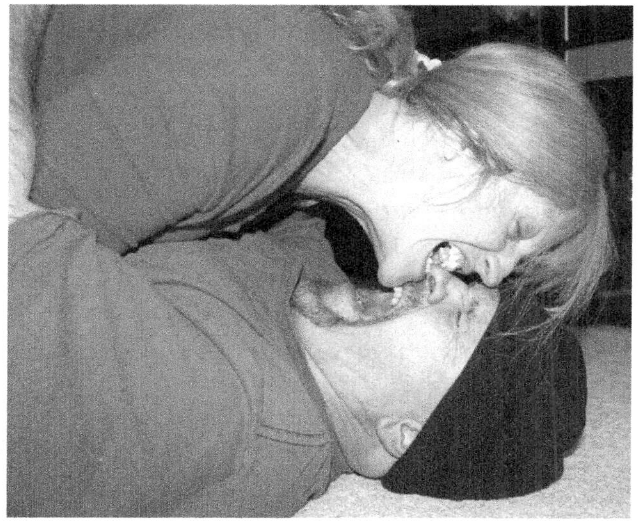

Sometimes a vicious counterattack is your only chance of survival.

(Photo courtesy of Loren W. Christensen and Lisa Place)

Your attacker will most likely be bigger, stronger, and more accustomed to violence. If he's a career criminal, he's done this before. You, on the other hand, might be experiencing your first act of violence. Fear will want to paralyze you, and adrenaline will be surging through your body, disrupting fine motor skills.

But if you've developed your fighter's mindset, you will react, and this reaction will be vicious. You must be able to direct the physical techniques you've learned in martial art or self-defense courses toward your attacker violently and aggressively to stop the attack and create an avenue of escape so you can get to safety.

> ***"Some martial artists teach you to love your enemy. I hate my enemy. When he attacks, I'm going to crush him – physically, spiritually and mentally – and I won't feel bad about it."***
>
> **- Kelly McCann**

If someone attacks you, he must be stopped at once, and completely. You cannot afford to give him a second chance. I don't care who he is, why he's a criminal, what his social background is, or what his ideological or psychological motivations are. All I care about is you staying alive. If you can avoid the confrontation, do so. If you can escape to safety, do so.

But when you are physically attacked, and your attacker means to do serious bodily injury to you, or worse yet, kill you, you must attack back aggressively, ruthlessly, and viciously. You must stop him without holding back. Once he is incapable of further action, stop, but see to it that he is stopped first.

> ***"While both moral and legal precepts enjoin us against so-***

> ***called "over-reaction," we are fully justified in valuing the life and person of an intended victim more highly than the life of a pernicious assailant."***
>
> **- Colonel Jeff Cooper**

The law forbids us from taking revenge, but it permits us to prevent others from harming or killing us. If the person is still a threat, you must do whatever it takes to prevent him from continuing his assault against you. Use no more force than necessary to accomplish this, but use all the force necessary to ensure he's stopped and you remain safe.

Watch the news, read the papers, and search the Internet for stories of criminals who prey upon innocent citizens. Get angry! They have no right to do this to others. They have no right to commit violence against you! These people are evil, and you are justified in becoming angry over their behavior and actions. Use this anger to cultivate your vicious response to an attack. Don't be afraid of hurting your attacker. Strike back with everything you have. Strike back viciously with intent to stop him anyway you must. When your life depends on it, there is no other way.

When your life is on the line, you must possess the ferocity of a tiger!

If someone attacks you, get angry. They have no right! Attack back with ruthless, aggressive viciousness and make them pay for choosing you as their next victim. That's the fighter's mindset that I want you to possess in the time of need.

Your life may depend on your ability to block out all thoughts other than those of destroying your enemy with complete viciousness. You must not allow an attacker to dominate your mind, will or body.

Decide right now that you will do whatever it takes to survive. Get angry at those who prey on others. You won't be a victim! You won't be a statistic. You have the fighter's mindset. If lethally attacked, you will be ruthless, aggressive and vicious.

"When it comes to mindset, train yourself to adhere to the

following principle: mentally prepare to react with a fighting rage when attacked."

- Bill Bryant Sr.

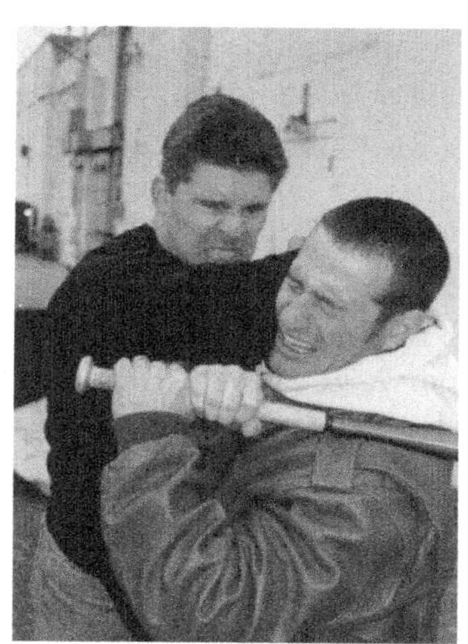

Elbows can be Vicious!

Be Determined
Refuse To Lose

During a violent attack, you must not accept defeat, even if the odds against you seem overwhelming due to the size, numbers or ferocity of the attack. One thing is certain, if you give up, give in, or surrender to your attacker, you will be at his (or their) mercy. That is a place I don't want to be, and I don't want you to be there either. Many criminals are merciless and I never want you to rely on their mercy for your safety and survival.

There are too many stories of people who have begged for their lives only to be killed by ruthless coldhearted criminals. We probably can't count the number of women who were told they wouldn't be harmed if they didn't resist and then were raped and brutally killed afterward. Never submit to your attacker. (Unless it is a fake, or a ploy, to get him to lower his guard so you can fight back or escape.) You will never surely know your attacker's intentions. But you must know your own, and your intentions are to be determined to survive, refuse to lose and do everything in your power to see to it that you defeat your attacker and get to safety.

And remember, if you sprint as fast as you can toward safety, immediately when recognizing the danger (Because you were alert and aware!), you have defeated your attacker. A "win" for you and a "lose" for him is any situation where you get to safety and he didn't get his way with you, whether his intentions were rape, murder or other mayhem.

Sometimes we fall into a mindset that the only "win" is crushing our enemy physically. This isn't realistic, and it fails to acknowledge our true goals. Our goal is to get home safe, or get our loved ones home safe. That does not mean you have to physically destroy your attacker. (While this may sound good, and we often wish this on those who prey on innocent victims, it is not realistic or practical.) Anything you can do to get to safety is a "win" for you. Sometimes you won't have to fight at all if you can sprint away from danger, do so. If it only takes minimal fighting to break free and then sprint away, do that.

However, if you are locked into mortal combat with an attacker who means to do you serious bodily injury or kill you, I want that mindset of winning, of refusing to lose, to be one that carries you through doing whatever is necessary to stop the person from harming you. And that means being aggressive, ruthless, and vicious as discussed earlier.

Do whatever you must to stop an attacker and then get to safety. Do not submit. Get angry at him for attacking you.

Be Determined!

Refuse to lose!

(Photo courtesy of Loren W. Christensen & Lisa Place)

For some people, this determination, refusal to quit, and the will to win comes more naturally. Some people just seem to be born with it. I know I was. From my earliest memories, I hated losing and always strove to win at everything I did. And while I developed good sportsmanship behavior and accept that I can't win at everything, I still hate losing and have that determination to win inside.

One of the reasons I think this is sometimes inherited, is because I see similar character traits in my daughter. Which I think is great when it comes to me teaching her to defend herself. It's not as good with other things, and my wife and I are teaching her to be a good sport, and that sometimes in games you don't always win.

I've taught her that I don't mind that she is upset when she loses, as long as she waits till she is in private to be upset. At the time of the game, she needs to congratulate the winner and her team mates if playing on a team, and only when she's alone can she be mad and upset over losing. And then she needs to take those feelings and practice harder and better herself for next time.

> ***"Winning is not a sometime thing, it is an all the time thing. You don't do things right once in a while… you do them right all the time."***
>
> **- Vince Lombardi**

Some might say I should teach her to not have those feelings, but I don't know if that is possible. We have feelings. They are natural. I'm teaching her to control those feelings and use them to make herself better. I don't want to eliminate them, just have her control them.

One of my favorite basketball players was Pistol Pete Maravich. (I wore number 23 when I played basketball because it was his number at LSU.) He also hated losing. That, and a rather demanding father, contributed to Maravich's almost obsessive practicing of basketball skills. That dedication and determination manifested into a successful high school and college basketball career and one of the first million dollar contracts in the NBA. So I don't mind my daughter being upset at losing, as long as she uses those feelings and emotions in a productive manner and displays good sportsmanship to others.

Peter "Pistol Pete" Press Maravich

(June 22, 1947 – January 5, 1988)

Pistol Pete from his days at LSU.

Another reason I think some of this is inherited is from an interview with Jaeson Maravich in 2003. (Jaeson was eight years old when Pete Maravich died unexpectedly at the age of 40 from a rare congenital defect; he had been born with a missing left coronary artery, a vessel which supplies blood to the muscle fibers of the heart. I was stationed at Fort Bragg when he died in January, 1988, and couldn't believe my basketball hero died at 40 years of age.) Anyway, Jaeson told *USA Today* that, when he was still only a toddler, "My dad passed me a (Nerf) basketball, and I've been hooked ever since… My dad said I shot and missed, and I got mad and I kept shooting. He said his dad told him he did the same thing."

After reading about Pistol Pete when I was young, and learning how he hated losing, would get mad, and then practice harder, I didn't feel as bad about my own feelings. And I don't feel bad about my daughter's, as long as I can help her learn to control them.

When it comes to being attacked, I am grateful for those feelings and am glad my daughter has them too. I've said many times that it was my physical conditioning and my determination to win that got me through many of the fights I was in when younger. (I also have written about and talked about how many of those were stupid and should have been avoided, but that is a topic for another time.) The important thing here is that determination and refusing to lose can help see you through a violent encounter. You must develop this part of mindset if you don't already possess it inherently.

You can do this by getting angry at those who do others harm, just like I discussed in the "Be Vicious" section. How dare criminals violate innocent victims? Become indignant of them. Get angry. Determine right now that you will never be a victim. You will not allow yourself to be intimidated by size or appearance. You will exploit all weakness of your attacker and savagely attack his vital areas.

You will fight hard, you will fight smart, you will fight to win. (Remember what winning means – get to safety!) You will be determined. You will refuse to lose!

> ***"Winning isn't everything. The will to win is the only thing."***
>
> **- Vince Lombardi**

Vincent Thomas "Vince" Lombardi
(June 11, 1913 – September 3, 1970)

Be Cool

If you can keep your head
When all about you
Are losing theirs
And blaming it on you…
If you can trust yourself
When all men doubt you…

- Rudyard Kipling

In this section, I want to discuss being cool. It's an important part of the fighter's mindset. Since I enjoy tough guy movies, I want you to think of John Travolta playing Chile Palmer. He was cool. Travolta played the role in both *Get Shorty* (1995) and the appropriately titled sequel, *Be Cool* (2005).

In fact, most movie tough guys are cool in the face of danger, that's part of what makes them tough guys. I mean, was Clint Eastwood ever not cool? It didn't matter what was happening, he was under control and in charge of himself: he was (and is) cool!

Sure, I'm talking movies right now, and this book is about real life. It's about real life and death seriousness in fact. However, I find movies good for illustrating and teaching lessons, as well as for motivation and of course, fun. So if you can role model your favorite hero, and if that helps you "be cool," why not?

Part of being cool is sometimes called arousal control, which reflects the degree to which you can control the effects of the adrenaline rush so that they do not interfere with your performance during what you must do.

Another part is controlling yourself so that you can choose the right response, which many times can be avoidance or de-escalation, rather than going physical. But it takes control to de-escalate situations, and it takes being cool.

Research actually shows that different people perform better at different states of arousal. It would behoove you to determine your optimal state before you must perform under severe conditions when the stakes are high. Find out what your optimal arousal level is to maximize your performance.

> ***"I don't psych myself up. I psych myself down. I think clearer when I'm not psyched up."***
>
> **- Racing Jockey Steve Cauthen**

Where do you perform best? Athletic competition can help you determine this for yourself. Do you get psyched up to get in the zone, or do you prefer a still calmness right before you must act. For a much more detailed look at arousal and its effect on performance as related to the fighter's mindset, I strongly recommend the book *Warrior Mindset: Mental Toughness Skills for a Nation's Peacekeepers.* It's listed in the suggested reading list near the end of this book.

While a certain arousal state can be positive in regards to performance, certain stress can have a negative influence on what we need to do to accomplish our mission, which in a self-defense situation is to not only survive, but to get home safe. Stress can disrupt a person by making them choke, freeze, maintain a "death grip," increase muscle tension and become fatigued, disrupt coordination, and blur one's vision. These are real physical disruptions caused by increased stress.

Additional perceptual distortions may occur, such as auditory exclusion or diminished sounds, intensified sounds, tunnel vision, heightened visual clarity, time distortion, memory related distortion, disassociation, intrusive distracting thoughts and temporary paralysis. These effects can profoundly affect your response in self-defense or emergency situation.

Joint-locking and other self-defense skills will deteriorate under stress, fear, and the adrenaline dump associated with fighting.

Through proper training, you can reduce these effects and use your skills to defend yourself.

Because fear and the state of arousal are natural, the key is to understand and manage these feelings or emotions, not try to prevent or eradicate them.

> ***"The ability to understand the dynamics of fear in such critical instances is the first step to controlling fear and using it to one's own advantage."***
>
> **- Roger Solomon**

You must learn how, and train yourself, to keep cool under pressure. Anger, as long as it is controlled anger, is okay. "Controlled" is the key here. You must have self-control. This is critical for many reasons when you are attacked.

First, you want to be cool and control the disruptions previously mentioned. Additionally, you must have your wits about you to select and execute the responses that will save you, but keep you from injuring yourself or injuring your opponent too much. (Remember, we also must think about the moral and legal repercussions of our actions.)

> ***"Understanding and recognizing the adrenal reaction and its physical and mental effects can bring us to actualize its very powerful positive value in stressful situations. This 'adrenal advantage' is not limited to physical self-defense either; it enters into every aspect of our lives."***
>
> **- Peyton Quinn**

During the heat of battle, punching an attacker in the midsection can be a good blow; punching him in the head with a closed fist can result in a broken hand, putting one of your weapons out of commission, and possibly not damaging your attacker near as much as a different technique such as a throat shot or eye jab could have done. You must be cool and under control to maximize your effectiveness.

Besides certain training methodologies such as adrenal stress training, certain athletics can help a person train to be calm under pressure. Football is one. All successful quarterbacks must be cool and calm under the pressure of huge linemen bearing down on them if they want to execute their play successfully.

But any sport that makes you perform under pressure can help train you to better react in emergencies. This is one reason I am so in favor of kids playing multiple sports as they grow up. Besides fun, character development, and working with a team, these activities help kids stay in shape and learn to handle themselves both physically and emotionally under pressure. And that is a great skill to have, not only for defending oneself.

Soccer is just one of the sports our daughter plays, and yes, it makes me proud to see her out in front after the ball. More proud to see her developing sportsmanship and the proper mindset.

Autogenic or "Combat" Breathing

I start out every Hapkido class with dan jun breathing, just like every class I trained in South Korea started. The dan jun is located about three inches below the navel, and is believed to be the center of energy (Qi or Ki) in the human body. The dan jun breathing exercises not only stimulate Ki, or energy, but help students locate and become aware of their center, where most Hapkido movements originate from for optimum effectiveness.

We do a series of breathing exercises and then move on to our other training. I always emphasize to my students that they should be doing some type of breathing exercise daily. Breathing is important for everything we do, and it is important for being cool and preparing yourself for combat, or to deal with other stressful or emergency situations too. Not to mention all of the health benefits associated with deep abdominal breathing and other various breathing exercises.

> ***"A big part of "proper mind" is a relaxed mind."***
>
> **- Peyton Quinn**

Besides my Hapkido dan jun breathing, I've studied breathing in other martial arts, including Qigong, techniques from motivational success guru Tony Robbins, techniques from doctors Gay Hendricks, Ph.D., Andrew Weil, M.D., and various other breathing methods and techniques from various other sources.

For the purposes of this book, I want to share a very simple breathing pattern that I learned from reading books by Lt. Col. Dave Grossman, Loren W. Christensen and Michael J. Asken, Ph.D. (You can find this in several of their books, and I also share this in my DVD *Restraint, Control & Come-A-Long Techniques Vol 2*.)

This is a simple four-count breathing pattern that is effective for slowing the thumping of your excited heartbeat, reducing the trembling of your hands and knocking of your knees, clearing your mind, and helping you stay calm, relaxed and in control.

The technical term is autogenic breathing, but many refer to it as tactical breathing or combat breathing. Many law enforcement officers use this when responding to a call or before a high-risk forced entry. Soldiers have used this to calm their minds and bodies before they go into battle, and again after the battle to come down from the adrenaline rush. Surgeons use this technique when operating and fine motor control is essential.

I've had people come up to me literally years after attending a safety presentation where I taught this technique and tell me they used it to help prepare for a speech they had to give, that it helped with an interview, and even that it helped keep them calm during an altercation that had potential to go violent, but they were able to stay calm and de-escalate the situation.

The key is to practice this, and practice it often, so you will be able to easily perform the sequence when you really need it.

The Four-Count Autogenic Breathing Pattern

Start by breathing in through your nose for a slow count of four, pulling your breath deep into your lower belly (dan jun for you martial artists). Hold the breath for a slow count of four, and then slowly exhale out your mouth for a count of four. Let your belly deflate as the air goes out. Hold empty for a slow count of four before repeating the process. Do it now with this guide:

Breathe in through your nose, two, three, four. Hold, two, three, four.

Exhale out your mouth, two, three, four.
Hold, two, three, four.

Breathe in through your nose, two, three, four. Hold, two, three, four.

Exhale out your mouth, two, three, four.
Hold, two, three, four.

Breathe in through your nose, two, three, four. Hold, two, three, four.

Exhale out your mouth, two, three, four.
Hold, two, three, four.

That was a cycle of three. For many people, this short three cycle pattern is enough to calm their minds and bodies. For some people, or for some situations, you may need four to six cycles to get the benefits. There is no magic number that works exactly for everyone. You need to practice it and see what works for you. Maybe you want to use a count of five rather than four. Great, go for it. If it works for you, that is all that matters.

Do practice it though. It really is a simple, but powerful, technique that can help you in many situations, but only if you practice. Don't wait until right before a stressful situation, or worse yet, the middle of a dangerous one, to try it out. Practice this breathing pattern daily to learn what works the best for you and to be able to calm yourself whenever you choose. Like all of our self-defense techniques, practice now so you can perform when you need to most.

I want to also mention that being cool is critical when using a firearm for self-defense. This book is on a fighter's mindset, and the principles are important regardless if you are defending yourself with empty hands or various weapons up to and including firearms. But keeping your cool is especially important with guns. If you must shoot, you must do so with precision, and the only way you are going to do that is by keeping your wits about you and remaining calm, relaxed and cool. And that takes a lot of practice!

Talk about being cool! Martin Cooper, Alain Burrese, Bob Orlando, Marc MacYoung and Peyton Quinn (2002)

"If you keep cool when you fight, you are less likely to make mistakes. Since your overall goal is to survive, I advise you to keep this in mind."

- Marc "Animal" MacYoung

Believe In Yourself

"The Strongest single factor in acquiring abundance is self-esteem: believing you can do it, believing you deserve it, believing you will get it."

- Jerry Gillies

This is pretty simple really, but it is critical to having a fighter's mindset. You must believe in yourself and your capabilities. You must believe that you can and will do whatever it takes to survive. You won't be a victim! You won't be a statistic! You will go home to your loved ones! It's crucial that you truly believe this. If you don't, start telling yourself right now until you do.

Sure, it's not quite that simple, but there is power in self-talk, and from this point forward I want you to talk to yourself in a positive manner. Don't put yourself down, don't criticize yourself, and don't allow others to do it either. You are as important as any other human being on the planet. Your life and well-being are as valuable as everyone else's. The first step in believing in your capabilities is believing in yourself and your own self-worth.

It is very sad that there are people out there that don't believe their lives are worth fighting for. That's just wrong! I'll tell you right now, if you are alive, you are worth it. No one has the right to do your harm or kill you. You have every right to defend yourself and your loved ones from serious bodily injury or death by doing everything in your power to stop them, up to killing the person who is trying to do the same to you. You must believe in yourself and that your life is worth it and that no one has the right to take that away from you. This means attack back!

And don't give me any of that "fighting back will get you killed" nonsense. Yes, I know that so called "experts" used to teach this. And while they may have been well-intentioned, their advice was totally misguided and wrong.

"A strong aura of confidence goes a long ways toward not becoming a victim."

- Loren W. Christensen & Lisa Place

(Photo courtesy of Loren W. Christensen & Lisa Place)

Most self-defense instructors today, and I am one of them, teach to fight back in most cases. Fighting back is more successful than not, and never would I tell anyone to just "take it" as used to be taught, especially to women. It drives me crazy just thinking about it. While there may be rare occasions when a victim should choose not to fight back, such as against overwhelming odds of a gang attack where a successful defense would almost be impossible, they are few and far between.

I can understand that a person might choose not to fight, and wait for an opportunity with better odds of success, and that might be a better choice. One might also make the choice to not resist or fight back when attempting to save a loved one. But for most situations, choosing to fight back is the best choice, and to do so one must believe their life is worth fighting for.

There are many resources out there that help people overcome self-doubt and gain more self-confidence, self-worth, and belief in their own abilities. If this is a weakness, get some help or get some training. The only thing holding you back is yourself. So do it!

> ***"It ain't what they call you, it's what you answer to."***
>
> **- W.C. Fields**

Once you believe that your life is worth fighting for, and worth hurting, or possibly killing, another human being for, you are on your way to believing in yourself and your abilities. Just like an athlete must enter a competition believing in victory, you must enter a fight or combat believing you will also be victorious. Only on this field, victory isn't a gold medal or trophy, it's going home alive.

With that definition, always remember that breaking free and escaping to someplace safe is a victory. If you can do so without injuring your attacker, so be it. But if you must hurt or kill someone to make it home alive, do so with everything needed to accomplish that goal. And believe in yourself and your capabilities to get it done. Or, if you're a Larry the Cable Guy fan, do whatever you got's to do to get 'er done. Just get 'er done!

> ***"You gain strength, courage and confidence by every experience in which you really stop to look fear in the face."***
>
> **- Eleanor Roosevelt**

If he's bigger, you can take him with your speed or technique. If he's stronger or more skillful, you're more vicious, aggressive and ruthless. If he's younger, you are more experienced and have more wisdom. Regardless of the situation, believe that you have the advantage and that you can accomplish your goal of getting to safety with the minimum amount of injury to your body. Belief in yourself is an important part of the fighter's mindset.

"I tell you that you must believe, with all your heart. You must cultivate this attitude of survival, of never giving up. You must have an enduring attitude of faith in yourself and your skills."

- Rodger Ruge

Be Nice

"Whoever fights monsters should see to it that in the process he doesn't become a monster."

- Friedrich Nietzsche

This is another lesson I shared in the book *Campfire Tales from Hell: Musings on Martial Arts, Survival, Bouncing, and General Thug Stuff* edited by Rory Miller, and featuring Marc MacYoung, Wim Demeere, Lawrence Kane, Barry Eisler, and many others (2012).

Being nice is an extremely important aspect of mindset. While much of what I wrote has to do with reacting to, and engaging in, physical violence, this simple principle, being nice, can prevent more altercations and violence than just about any other. Many violent acts occur because one person makes another angry and they take out that anger with physical violence.

A friend of mine, who is a self-defense instructor, once responded to a person who claimed to have been in multiple altercations, "What are you doing to make so many people mad at you?" The simple fact is: being a jerk can get you punched, and being nice, or polite, can keep you out of physical altercations and a whole lot of other trouble. Here is a short story of how I used "being nice" to prevent a fight when I was working security one night.

I was wet. I was cold. And I wasn't happy that the band wasn't playing. The big differences between me and the angry crowd were I was sober, and I was being paid to be there. I liked the band, and had been looking forward to hearing them, but the main reason I wasn't happy that they weren't playing was that it just made my job more difficult.

It was an outdoor Black Crowes concert in Montana. I was working security when an unexpected wind and rain storm blew in. While the roof over the stage would protect from a straight downpour, the open sides did nothing to protect the sound equipment from the horizontal rain blowing in with the severe winds. While some people were busy trying to keep fences, tables, and portable outhouses from blowing away, I was assigned to keep people from hurting each other and to keep away from the stage.

Besides not wanting any of the angry mob to damage the stage or equipment, we had a legitimate concern with lightening being attracted by the metal structure and wanted to keep people safe from the additional potential danger. I was sure the show was not going to go on, but they hadn't made any kind of official announcement to the crowd. This lack of communication from the band and producers was only making the situation worse. Did I mention I wasn't happy?

I noticed an individual who was both large and loud. The way he was yelling and behaving had the potential to incite the already angry crowd toward a situation where people would get hurt. I thought, "Shit" to myself, as I started through the crowd toward him. It was my job to keep people and property from being hurt or damaged. As I neared him, I noticed the tattoos on his rather large guns bulging under the tight t-shirt. "Great, a former Marine," I thought. Alcohol must have been keeping him warm.

As I approached, I tried to keep Patrick Swayze's lessons from the movie *Road House* in mind. I've always liked tough guy movies, and that one had it all. Cinema masterpiece? No. But it sure was a fun tough guy movie, and it actually had a few tidbits of good advice. Swayze's character Dalton provided some good advice in the speech he gave to the Double Deuce employees when he took over as cooler:

> ***"All you have to do is follow three simple rules. One, never underestimate your opponent. Expect the unexpected. Two, take it outside. Never start anything inside the bar unless it's absolutely necessary. And three, be nice."***
>
> **- Patrick Swayze as Dalton,**
> ***Road House* (1989)**

It was the third rule, be nice, that I was especially trying to remember. This is actually a very good rule when bouncing or working security. Your demeanor, especially being nice, can prevent an awful lot of trouble and violence. Swayze continued his lesson in the movie by saying, "I want you to be nice, until it's time not to be nice." This too is an important consideration, and those who work in security need to understand when each is appropriate.

The former Marine noticed me approaching as the crowd around him started to part when they recognized I was moving toward the largest and loudest of them. He squared himself and puffed out his chest a bit. "The boy knows a weight room," I thought to myself.

Arrogantly, he said, "You're gonna need a lot more friends, and that flashlight ain't gonna help you." I was on my own at the moment, and I silently commended him for noticing the D-cell Maglight in my cargo pocket. It was at this very moment that I had a choice. And I had to make the choice instantly. I could puff up my own chest and come back with something to the effect of, "It's not me that needs more friends." Selecting this choice would almost certainly guarantee that things went physical. Not really the best alternative when you are being paid to prevent such occurrences. Or, I could choose to be nice. I choose the latter.

I continued toward him in a non-threatening manner. I think this surprised him a bit, because he was really expecting me to respond aggressively like my choice number one.

I walked up to him, placed my left hand on his shoulder in a friendly gesture, and said, "You're my friend, aren't you buddy?" He didn't really know what to say. I continued, "See all these people; I'm just trying to make sure no one gets hurt. I'm as pissed about the rain and band as you are. Also, I see you were a Marine. I was 82nd Airborne and a sniper instructor with the 2nd Infantry Division. Thank you for your service."

I held out my hand. He accepted it, and as we shook hands he said, "Thank you for your service too." We talked a few minutes more, everything was cool, and I left to deal with others. He wasn't a problem the rest of the night.

Working security provides ample opportunities to meet interesting people. Unfortunately, often at their worst.

Fortunately, the night wasn't much longer, because shortly after I spoke with him they made the official announcement that the concert was cancelled due to the water damaged equipment, and people would be able to get a refund the following week from whatever venue they purchased tickets from. The crowd then dispersed.

Because this principle is so important, especially when working in positions of security, law enforcement, bouncing and any related fields, I also told this story in my DVD *Restraint, Control & Come-A-Long Techniques Vol. 1.*

Far too many physical altercations could be prevented if instead of being aggressive, people would simply be nice. And while natural for some, it really is a learned response for others. Learning to be nice, even when you sometimes don't want to, is a valuable skill when dealing with aggressive behavior and wanting to prevent physical violence.

Does it work one hundred percent of the time? Of course not. But then, nothing does. However, being nice first does allow you to defuse and prevent many situations before things get out of hand. And you can always go from being nice, to not being nice, if you have to. But you can't go the other way. If you start out not being nice, you can't back up and change to being nice. It's too late, and you've already blown that opportunity. So if you don't want to take it from me when developing your fighter's mindset, take it from Patrick Swayze as Dalton, "I want you to be nice, until it's time not to be nice."

> ***"Polite is not the same as meek or timid."***
>
> **- Rory Miller**

Final Thoughts

The reason I write, speak, teach and practice the awareness, safety, and self-defense I write, speak, and teach about. Cosette & Yi-saeng Burrese California, 2007.

As I conclude this guide to developing your fighter's mindset, I want to include a brief warning. While it is true that you need the mindset contained in this guide to better be able to protect yourself, I would be shortchanging you if I didn't briefly include a brief section on responding with an appropriate response.

Sometimes when people get emotional, and it is easy to become emotional when dealing with a scary encounter, they may perceive dangers that are not actually there. This is important, because in the legal realm, self-defense is a defense claiming you were justified to use the amount of force used against another human being. Your responses must be appropriate to the level of danger you faced.

> ***"Before anything bad happens, preferably years before, you should become familiar with the legal aspects of self-defense – how much force you can legally use, when you can use it, and when to stop."***
>
> **- Sgt. Rory Miller**

I'm not going to go into the legalities of self-defense in this book (Hmm, topic for another book at another time?), but I encourage you to further research this topic, as it is important to your overall safety and self-defense strategy. You must be able to defend yourself on the street and in the courtroom. I don't want anything taking me away from my family: an attacker or a judge and jury. Make sure you think the same.

More Thoughts

Throughout this book, I've included wisdom from other experts on the topics I've discussed. You'll be able to find a list of titles that I referred to in the "Suggested Reading" portion of this book to further your education in defending yourself. But before that list, I want to include a few more quotes for you to enjoy and learn from. Here they are:

"Martial arts are something you do with someone; combatives you do to someone."

- Kelly McCann

"When everything is on the line, every man and woman has a storehouse of power available to use. You only have to aim everything you have – mental and physical – at escape."

- Stanford Strong

"Simply stated, awareness is a blend of two things. One is being in touch with your external and internal environment; the second is knowing what things mean in that particular place (sometimes referred to as 'knowing how things work 'round here'')."

- Marc "Animal" MacYoung

"True combat firearms training is based upon teaching students to fire at a human opponent who is exhibiting a life threatening stimulus. Without this type of stimulus, trainers cannot expect their students to respond automatically and accurately in their first combat experience."

- Bruce K. Siddle

"In your own mind, you must always believe that you and you

alone will prevail – that you will win and not die."

- Larry Jordan

"Self-control is the means by which the fighter suppresses his fear or channels his fear into anger. Uncontrolled fear and anger will clean you out in a hurry and leave you shaking like a leaf. Successful athletes, soldiers, and criminals know how to keep the lid on the rage so they can apply sustained aggression, thereby reserving the ability to go berserk, if necessary."

- James LaFond

"Determine right now that you will not be the victim. Say to yourself, 'Heaven help the poor guy who tries anything funny with me!' Take offense every time you are offended."

- Lt. Jim Bullard

"The first line of self-defense is your ability to practice using your awareness skills, trusting your intuition, and not discounting eerie feelings that may come over you in certain places or situations. Trust your feelings. If it feels wrong, it probably is. And even if your suspicions are wrong, at least you are noting your environment in ways that help to keep you vigilant, aware and safe."

- David Loshelder, M.S.Ed.

"Use of countervailing force is an individual decision based on each unique situation, taking into account legal, moral, ethical, religious, and psychological considerations."

- Lawrence A. Kane

"If you believe you will survive no matter what happens, you probably will."

- Bill Kipp

"You can learn a lot in training, but the main thing you'll need to develop is the streetfighter mentality, for once you're committed to a physical conflict, you have no choice but to go all the way."

- Massad Ayoob

"The instant you catch a glimpse of a weapon (knife, gun, bat, etc.), assuming it is not yet touching you and you are not yet restrained, RUN (or hit the gas)!"

- John Perkins, Al Ridenhour, & Matt Kovsky

"Martial art training breeds a level of confidence that springs only from the knowledge that you are not easily threatened or intimidated. In the street or in the board room, you now have choices. Untrained, you have no choice but submission.

Trained, you choose whether to yield or stand your ground. This kind of choice is available only to those who first choose to study martial arts."

- Bob Orlando

"In a life-threatening attack, it is your thoughts, attitude, and actions that will decide the outcome, not those of the attacker. If you don't seek to win, you subconsciously accept defeat and all that comes with it, including death."

- Larry Jordan

"The Most decisive element will often be the mind-set of the combatants rather than their weapons, 'technical skill,' or anything else."

- Peyton Quinn

"A key ingredient in any survival situation is the mental attitude of the individual involved."

- Department of the Army
Field Manual 3-05.70

"Pay attention to everything that is going on around you; the time you spend in la-la land is the time you are most likely to get hurt."

- Bill Bryant Sr.

"To survive, you must be able to face life-altering events in a moment's notice and without the slightest hesitation…Mental exercise is at least as important as physical exercise and skill building when it comes to enhancing your performance in crisis situations."

- Rodger Ruge

"In the end, it is not about the 'hardware,' it is about the 'software.' Amateurs talk about hardware or equipment, professionals talk about software or training and mental readiness."

- Lt. Col. David Grossman

"There are people who have difficulty actually hitting someone. I guess it's because of some cultural conditioning against violence. I must admit this is something of a mystery to me, but I know this attitude exists. Regardless of whether the circumstances call for violent action, some people will hesitate. This is disastrous. You must not trap yourself into this disabling mind-set. Since you cannot fix something until you know what is wrong, examine your own spirit for this problem. Don't discover it in a fight. It will be too late."

- Peyton Quinn

"In a real fight you must win. Second place results in death. If you have to fight it is all or nothing."

- John Perkins, Al Ridenhour, & Matt Kovsky

"Learn to use your fear! Don't fight it! Fear is one of your greatest allies. If you learn how to channel it, you can use it to defeat your foe instead of letting it defeat you. Most fights aren't lost because of skill or strength, most fights are lost because of fear."

- Marc "Animal" MacYoung

"My men don't surrender. I don't want to hear of any soldier under my command being captured unless he has been hit. Even if you are hit, you can still fight back."

- General George S. Patton, Jr.

General George Smith Patton, Jr.
(11/11/1885 – 12/21/1945)

"America's Fightingest General"

Suggested Reading

The following books taught me many valuable lessons that help me with my training, teaching, and speaking. (Not to mention the personal protection measures I live by.) They also helped me with writing *How To Protect Yourself By Developing A Fighter's Mindset.*

There are amazon links to all of these books that are available on amazon from this book's main page:

http://burrese.com/how-to-protect-yourself-by-developing-a-fighters-mindset

Asken, Michael J.; Grossman, David with Christensen, Loren. ***Warrior Mindset***
Ayoob, Massad. ***The Truth About Self-Protection***
Bryant, Bill Sr. ***Strictly Street Stuff***
Bullard, Jim. ***Looking Forward To Being Attacked***
Christensen, Loren W. ***Defensive Tactics***
Christensen, Loren W. and Place, Lisa. ***Fight Back***
Cooper, Jeff. ***Principles of Personal Defense***
Grossman, David with Christensen, Loren. ***On Combat***
Jordan, Larry. ***The Dirty Dozen***
Kane, Lawrence A. ***Surviving Armed Assaults***
Kane, Lawrence A. and Wilder, Kris. ***The Little Black Book Of Violence***
Kipp, Bill. ***Turning Fear Into Power***
LaFond, James. ***The Fighting Edge***
Loshelder, David. ***Protect Yourself***

MacYoung, Marc. ***Cheap Shots, Ambushes, and Other Lessons***
MacYoung, Marc ***A Professional's Guide To Ending Violence Quickly***
MacYoung, Marc. http://www.nononsenseselfdefense.com
MacYoung, Marc. ***Taking It To The Street***
McCann, Kelly. ***Combatives For Street Survival***
Miller, Rory. ***Facing Violence***
Miller, Rory. ***Meditations On Violence***
Miller, Rory, and others. ***Campfire Tales From Hell: Musings on Martial Arts, Survival, Bouncing, and General Thug Stuff***
Orlando, Bob. ***Martial Arts America***
Perkins, John; Ridenhour, Al; Kovsky, Matt. ***How To Fight For Your Life***
Quinn, Peyton. ***A Bouncer's Guide To Barroom Brawling***
Quinn, Peyton. ***Freedom From Fear***
Quinn, Peyton. ***Real Fighting***
Ruge, Roger. ***The Warrior's Mantra***
Siddle, Bruce K. ***Sharpening The Warrior's Edge***
Strong, Sanford. ***Strong On Defense***
Suarez, Gabe. ***The Combative Perspective***

"Books are what you step on to take you to a higher shelf. The higher your stack of books, the higher the shelf you can reach."

– Jim Rohn

About the Author

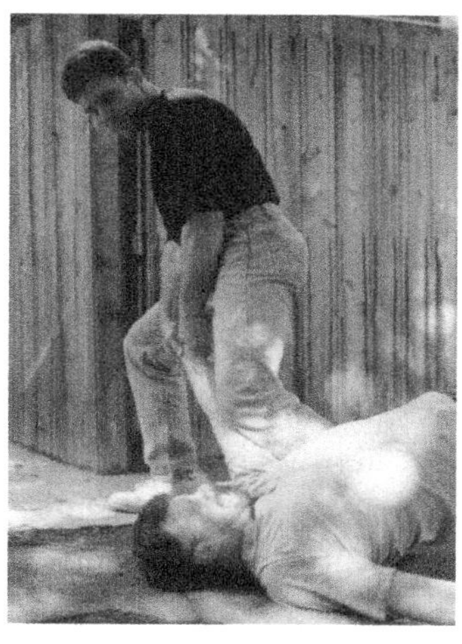

Alain Burrese performing a joint-lock on Frank Spears.

(R.I.P. Buddy)

Alain Burrese started his martial art training with Fred Neff and Bruce Tegner books in the 1970s. It was before *The Karate Kid* came out, but Alain was doing the same thing, following along with the books, learning what he could. In 1982, Alain had his first formal training in Judo, an art he studied and competed in during high school. The Judo foundation served him well for real encounters and further training in other arts throughout the years.

As he moved around in the military and after, he studied at various Karate, Taekwondo, Judo, and Hapkido schools. Of the arts he studied, Hapkido, especially because of the joint locks and the use of a cane as a weapon, was the art he most enjoyed. (Yes, he admits he was influenced by *Billy Jack* and *The Trial of Billy Jack* that featured Hapkido Grand Master Bong Soo Han. And it was a great pleasure when he had the opportunity to meet and train with Grandmaster Han at his school in Santa Monica before he passed away.)

Alain furthered his training in Hapkido by moving to Korea to train in the home country of the self-defense art. He paid the bills by teaching English which provided him the opportunity to live and train there. He attended two classes a day and one on Saturday while living in Korea. On subsequent visits, he'd train four classes a day and some in between. He continues to go back to train with his instructors and visit family and friends when he can, and plans on arranging Warrior's Edge tours so others can experience the wonders of this Asian country.

Alain with Hapkido instructor Lee Jun-kyu, South Korea

Alain's military background includes two years as a paratrooper with an Infantry Battalion in the 82nd Airborne Division at Fort Bragg, N.C., and working as a sniper instructor at the 2nd Infantry Division Scout Sniper School at Camp Casey, South Korea. (The military tour was his first time living in Korea, and he has also lived in Japan and toured other Asian countries.)

Additionally, Alain has always focused on practical self-defense. While in the Army, he found himself in a number of fights and brawls, while at the same time he started learning from people like Marc "Animal" MacYoung and Peyton Quinn. At the time, he didn't know he'd become friends and teach alongside the two and many other notable martial art and self-defense instructors.

During his entire life, Alain has always studied and practiced the ways of the warrior. While his focus for a martial art is primarily Hapkido, he studies from all arts and self-defense systems. He also studies warrior concepts and how they apply to life as well as the battlefield.

Alain Burrese with Hapkido instructor Kim Hyun, South Korea

Alain's formal education includes a Bachelor's Degree in Business Administration with a Management Emphasis and a Communication Studies Minor, and a Juris Doctor Degree from The University of Montana School of Law. Besides these, he has extensive training in Negotiation and Dispute Resolution. You can find out more about these areas and the trainings he does at his personal site http://burrese.com.

Alain continues to train in the Korean art of Hapkido, and he teaches an on-going class in Montana. He also teaches seminars on joint locks, the cane for self-defense, safety, self-defense, and various other martial topics. Beyond that, he also teaches how to live with The Warrior's Edge. He helps people find their Warrior's Edge to live more powerfully with honor, integrity, and the decisiveness and determination found among warriors.

He currently lives in Montana with his wife and daughter, where he trains, teaches, writes and speaks. He has a number of book, DVD, and audio projects in the works.

STREETFIGHTING ESSENTIALS Combining Western Boxing and Hapkido into an Unstoppable Self-Defense System

Developing a Fighter's Mindset is crucial to protecting yourself, but it's not everything. You also want to learn and train in physical self-defense techniques that will save you when attacked. *Streetfighting Essentials* is a 2 disc DVD set that will do just that – teach you self-defense techniques that will save you if attacked!

Streetfighting Essentials
2 Disc Set – 150 minutes - $29.95
You can't find a better self-defense program for the price anywhere!

http://burrese.com/streetfighting-essentials

Streetfighting Essentials Reviews

The following review was written by Loren W. Christensen, author of nearly 50 books on self-defense and police science, in 2002. The review was originally written for a law enforcement magazine, but can also be found on amazon.com.

In the two-disc set, *Streetfighting Essentials: Combining Western Boxing and Hapkido into an Unstoppable Self-defense System*, veteran martial arts trainer Alain Burrese teaches you basic hand strikes, footwork, low-line kicks, escapes from chokes, grabs, bear-hugs, and other essentials to help you come out on top of the most violent confrontations, so that you end your shift just as healthy and pretty as you began.

Alain draws on his extensive background in judo and Hapkido, as well as his in-the-trenches experience in the military and working as a bodyguard and bouncer in some of the toughest locations around the world. He packages his knowledge in an organized presentation that benefits the novice as well as the seasoned fighter.

In Disc One, Alain shows the precise way to stand, move, block, and execute the classic jab, cross, hook and uppercut, all combined with well-balanced footwork. After he demonstrates the best target for each punch, he introduces the palm-heel strike to use with the aforementioned punches, which is a better choice for officers so as to prevent injury to their gun hands. He goes on to teach several other hand strikes

– including some designed to stop an assailant but not seriously hurt him – and a half dozen simple kicks.

Alain doesn't waste time and videotape with fancy smancy techniques that have little or no street application. Probably because of his background of fighting for real, he sticks to solid basics, the precise techniques needed by street officers when wristlocks are not enough. Realistic street attack scenarios are interspersed throughout the lessons to show how the presented material works in the mean streets.

In Disc Two, Alain teaches how to escape from a large variety of common grabs and holds, information rare to find in any police academy. There is a section on how to fall properly, and another section that teaches you how to execute a few basic throws, drags, head twists, and pull-downs. Even if you are well versed in self-defense, there will be something for you in these videos.

Streetfighting Essentials: Combining Western Boxing and Hapkido into an Unstoppable Self-defense System is designed for, as Alain says, "the person who does not want to study martial arts for years… and to help the martial artist who wants to cross the boundary into real self-defense situations."

Does he accomplish his objective? Yes, he does, and the excellent camera work and interspersed, realistic scenarios all add up to a high quality DVD set applicable to the needs of law enforcement.

The following review was written by Tim B. on amazon.com in January, 2012. It is also listed as a "verified purchase" on amazon.

This very affordable 2 DVDR self-defense package was released in 2002 by Paladin Press and Alain Burrese (pronounced: Alan Burr-ee-se.) At that time Alain had been a Martial Artist for 18 years. Korean Hapkido, a Martial Art with emphasis on Self-Defense, is what Alain references for this set.

Alain served in the U.S. Military, and has performed security and bodyguard work since leaving the military. Besides producing several videos, he is also an author, and e-book author. Alain authored the hard-to-find book *Hard Won Wisdom*, and recently an e-book, or traditional print, series called *Tough Guy Wisdom*. He also produced the videos *Hapkido Hoshinsul*, *Hapkido Cane* and the *Lock On Joint Locking Essentials* series.

This set was designed for the person that doesn't want to study a Martial Art for years. Period. Alain distills his Hapkido art down to the essentials necessary to help you learn self-defense for use on the street, and it will also will help the dedicated Martial Artist cross-over to learn real Self-Defense versus what he or she may practice in the dojo.

Alain has done a great job of presenting a lot of material that is easily learned, easy to understand, and likely to save your bacon when the heat gets turned up.

DVD1:

In Chapter ONE Alain introduces a very important principle that is your best defense against in any situation - awareness. We are all way too caught up in our cell phones and other personal electronic devices and we tend to lose track of what else is going on all around us. That leaves us vulnerable to attack. The first thing you'll learn here is to become more aware of what's going on around you, at all times. Failing to do so will present someone else with the opportunity to relieve you of your belongings, simple as that.

Chapter TWO teaches you proper stance and footwork. Alain explains stance and how to move your feet to maintain balance and proper positioning. The moves and principles are again easily acquired. Alain goes on to demonstrate some simple scenarios of how to implement these movements in relation to facing a potential aggressor.

In Chapter THREE is Alain describes over a dozen strikes that can be used on the upper-body of an aggressor. Alain demonstrates a strike and then an upper-body target and explains why the particular strike/target will work.

Chapter FOUR is about lower-body strikes/targets. Again, Alain presents suitable strikes and targets.

DVD 2:

This dvd starts with some common grabs and chokes that you may fall victim to. These techniques may also be used against larger and/or stronger aggressors, which makes them very useful.

Chapter TWO is dedicated to break-falls - learning how to fall properly, and safely. Alain demonstrates a few ways to ease yourself into these techniques. Learning how to fall and recover will be very important in your overall study.

In Chapter THREE is a brief study about being or ending up on the ground, while being attacked by an aggressor. You don't want to end up there! Alain shows you a few very effective strikes that will fend off an attacker and perhaps present you with the opportunity to regain your feet.

Chapter FOUR ties it all together. Alain demonstrates a few combinations and encourages you to create and practice your own. All attacks are different, and how you choose to defend against them will never be the same twice. In some other systems, these are known as flow-drills.

This is a great DVD set that will help most anyone - students, martial artists, security personnel, healthcare professionals, and anyone that wants to have more confidence when facing a threat. Alain's style is very easy to watch and learn from, the audio and video are topnotch, and there's a lot of great material here.

Being a healthcare professional I found many techniques that I will recommend that our institution consider in our training regimen. Do yourself a favor and buy this very affordable set - you're sure to learn something new, useful, and most of all - effective!

The following review was written by Thomas O. Morrison on amazon.com, August, 2007.

I just watched Alain Burrese's *STREETFIGHTING ESSENTIALS - Combining Western Boxing and Hapkido into an Unstoppable Self-Defense System* 2-DVD set and was very impressed at what I saw.

In his introduction, Mr Burrese explains that this set is for a basic set of essential techniques for self-defense. He offers some good basic striking (hands and feet) combined with the goal to "streamline Hapkido into the bare essentials for the street, crossing the line into 'real' self-defense." The hallmark of all of Mr Burrese's DVDs is thoroughness and systematic development of the material, and this set hold true to that as well.

As it stands, this set would be an ideal base to create a self-defense core system "add-on" to another art (like Taekwondo or etc.). There is a lot of room here to modify, adapt and fit it into what you do.

Students who want "more" could look to flesh this out in several ways, either through cross training or other sources. To be honest, this reminds me a lot of the basic few levels of "Combat Hapkido", with much of the same attitude, ideas, philosophy, and even techniques. Interested students who like this set would probably be happy to build further on it through Combat Hapkido (ICHF). Alternatively, students who wanted the more traditional side would find this a decent introduction to Traditional Hapkido as well (especially if they looked at Mr Burrese's other DVD offerings).

The set is made up of two disks, for a total of about 2 and a half hours of material. Each section is very thorough with a wide range of demonstrations, tips on performance and targets, and everything is tied together well. There are nice review sections at the end of each section which show all of the techniques in short order.

Interspaced throughout the disks are self-defense scenarios showing Alain (and others) defending against attackers in realistic settings. The normal clothes and outdoor settings add a hint of realism and the responses are very well put together, very realistic.

The details:

Disk 1

Introduction - including a great bit on awareness and avoidance.

The first 20 minutes covers a neutral stance, basic footwork/movement, positioning, blocks and slipping attacks. At the end of this section, there is a quick and easy review of the material covered. (This type of review follows each section and was very useful)

The next 36 minutes covered upper body strikes, ranging from basic jabs, crosses, hooks, and uppercuts to hammer fists, and knife hands to palm strikes, forearm strikes and elbows. All are demonstrated with careful attention to footwork, power generation, targeting and practicality.

The last 25 minutes of this disk covers a range of lower body strikes ranging from basic kicks (front, side, roundhouse) to practical ones like stomps, scoop kicks, and knees. There is also a short section on head butts and biting(!). Again, everything is demonstrated with careful attention to footwork, power generation, targeting and practicality.

Disk 2

The first 35 minutes of this disk shows breakaways, escapes, throws, and other ways to deal with a variety of attacks ranging from wrist grabs, sleeve grabs, chokes, and lapel grabs to bear hugs, headlocks, nelsons and so on. Although there is only 1 or 2 techniques shown for each category, it should be noted that all of the various techniques can be cross-applied to the other categories, making for a wide range of effective responses.

Joint locks are not covered and he makes a reference that they are covered in a separate volume (although I would be more inclined to invest in Mr. Burrese's upcoming 5-volume set of *Lock On* joint lock instructional DVDs - excellent stuff.)

The next 20 minutes covers basic break falls and covers them well. I particularly enjoyed this section as it reminded me of almost exactly the same way I learned them in Korea. The next 10 minutes applies those falls in teaching sweeps, throws and takedowns.

The next section was the only disappointing section for me. The "Fighting on the Ground" section was only 7 minutes long and covered ideas on getting back up, kicking from the ground and escaping from a simple mount. The main idea was to avoid going to the ground, which I agree with but would have liked to have seen some more in depth takedown defenses (especially against someone with half-decent takedown skills) and a few more techniques to deal with being on the ground, e.g. escaping a guard or mount and getting back to your feet (or finishing on the ground). This section is the only part I wasn't completely satisfied with, but this is an area where you can get some supplemental material for to round out the system.

The final 8 minutes wraps up with a ideas on how to "combine the tools", showing some excellent combinations and scenarios. His basic principle is to finish quickly and get out of there. He reiterates that this "doesn't cover everything - it's just a core of essential techniques."

All in all, this is an excellent resource with a lot of great ideas and material to consider. Traditional HKD students may not see a lot of "new material" in it but may enjoy some of the different striking involved as well the tips and ideas on applying/combining material for street self-defense. For Combat Hapkido students, the same holds true although most of the physical material would have been covered by Green or Purple Belt in the ICHF curriculum.

http://burrese.com/streetfighting-essentials

DVDs by Alain Burrese

Do you want to learn to defend yourself with a common everyday item that you can even take aboard airplanes with you? The cane or walking stick is the ideal self-defense tool.

Growing in popularity as a defensive weapon with courses such as *Cane Fu*, people are recognizing they don't have to live in fear when they can legally carry a cane. You can take it anywhere, and once you learn the basics, you can defend yourself against all kinds of aggressive attacks. Learn to defend yourself with the cane today!

"This DVD set is well worth every penny. Its clear instructions, excellent photography and teaching methods are to be admired."

- P.J. De Maziere

In this 2-disc set, Alain Burrese shows you how to maximize the combative use of the cane, turning it from just a leg support to an invaluable part of your arsenal.

Available at: http://burrese.com/hapkido-cane

Lock On: Joint Locking Essentials series:

Wrist Locks

Arm Bars

Shoulder Locks

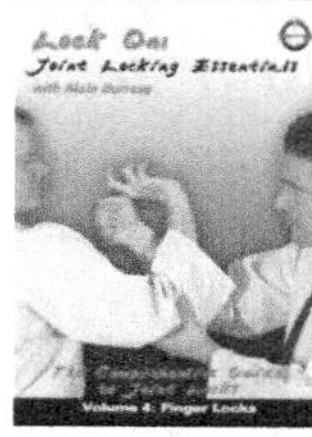

Finger Locks

Lock Flow Drills

Available at: http://burrese.com/dvds

"I knew many of the techniques Alain shows. With those I did know, I learned new nuances that made the familiar technique hurt even more. The ones I didn't know, Alain explained the steps so well that I was able to stand up and apply the move perfectly the first time. That's how well-taught these techniques are."

- Loren W. Christensen, author of nearly 50 books

"Alain Burrese shows a variety of arm locks with great skill and flair. The pacing of the DVD is perfect, with basic demonstrations first, followed by the small details that often make the difference between a technique working really well and not so well."

- Goran Powell, author of *A Sudden Dawn*

"Burrese moves well, explains clearly, demonstrates effectively, and ensures that viewers truly understand the materials. While no DVD is a substitute for hands-on instruction, this one is so good that it's the next best thing to being there. This is solid, practical instruction."

- Lawrence A. Kane, author of *Surviving Armed Assaults* & others

"Mr. Burrese has done an excellent job and I commend him fully."

- David Schultz

Made in the USA
Middletown, DE
28 February 2021

34532223R00076